AIR FRYER Favorites!

Publications International, Ltd.

Appliance photograph on front cover © Shutterstock.com.

Pictured on the front cover *(top to bottom):* French Toast Sticks *(page 8),* Italian-Style Roasted Vegetables *(page 150)* and Garlic Air-Fried Fries *(page 162).*

Pictured on the back cover *(top to bottom):* Chicken Air-Fried Steak with Creamy Gravy *(page 118),* Chicken Parmesan Sliders *(page 86)* and Chocolate Orange Lava Cakes *(page 182).*

ISBN: 978-1-64558-000-0

Manufactured in China.

8 7 6 5 4 3 2 1

Microwave Cooking: Microwave ovens vary in wattage. Use the cooking times as guidelines and check for doneness before adding more time.

Let's get social!
 @Publications_International
 @PublicationsInternational
www.pilbooks.com

CONTENTS

INTRODUCTION

It seems like everyone is air frying these days—with good reason! The air fryer not only makes delicious, crispy, crunchy—and often healthier—food, but it also makes everyday cooking quicker and easier.

Now you can find the best air fryer recipes all in one place—more than 110 recipes for any time of day, from breakfast to dessert and everything in between. Use your air fryer for a wide variety of dishes, including appetizers, snacks, sandwiches, vegetables and so much more. Homemade bagels and chocolate sticky buns are two of the impressive but easy air fryer breakfast options. Chicken wings, egg rolls and potato skins are guaranteed crowd pleasers you can make with minimal time and mess. Try quesadillas and wraps for quick-to-fix lunches, or cook juicy burgers, chicken and pork chop dinners in no time—they're all easier with an air fryer!

Helpful Tips

- Read the manufacturer's directions for your air fryer carefully before cooking to make sure you understand the specific settings and features of your machine.

- Preheat your air fryer for 2 to 3 minutes before cooking.

- To avoid foods sticking to your air fryer basket, use nonstick cooking spray or cook on parchment paper or foil. Spraying food occasionally with nonstick cooking spray during the cooking process will also help food to brown and crisp more easily.

- Don't overfill your basket. Smaller air fryers may require cooking food in several batches. Some foods should be cooked in a single layer for best results (as noted in the recipes), so cook these items in batches as needed. Crowding the basket will prevent foods from crisping and browning evenly.

- Use toothpicks to hold food in place. Sometimes light foods may blow around from the pressure of the fan, such as the top of a quesadilla or the top slice of bread in a sandwich. Securing foods in the basket with toothpicks can prevent this from happening.

- Check foods during cooking and turn the food or shake the basket for even browning, if necessary. This will not affect cooking times—once you return the basket, the cooking (and the timing) resumes.

- Experiment with cooking times of various foods, as different models of air fryers may cook slightly faster and cooking times can vary. Test foods for doneness before serving them; check meats and poultry with a meat thermometer, and use a toothpick to test muffins and cupcakes.
- Use a foil sling to get cake pans or baking dishes in and out of the air fryer basket. Fold a 24-inch piece of foil into a 2-inch-wide strip; place the pan in the center and use the ends to hold and raise or lower the dish into the air fryer. Tuck the ends down while cooking so the drawer can close.
- You can use your air fryer to cook foods typically prepared in the oven. But because the air fryer is more condensed than a regular oven, it is recommended that you reduce the temperature by 25°F to 50°F and reduce the cooking time by 20 percent when converting standard oven recipes to the air fryer.
- Use your air fryer to cook frozen foods, too! Frozen French fries, fish sticks, chicken nuggets, individual pizzas—these all work wonderfully in the air fryer. Just remember to reduce the cooking temperatures and times as recommended above.

Estimated Cooking Temperatures/Times*

FOOD	TEMPERATURE	TIMING
Beef (ground beef)	370°F	15 to 17 min.
Beef (steaks)	390°F	10 to 15 min.
Chicken (bone-in)	370°F	20 to 25 min.
Chicken (boneless)	370°F	12 to 15 min.
Fish	390°F	10 to 12 min.
Frozen Foods	390°F	10 to 15 min.
Pork	370°F	12 to 15 min.
Vegetables (asparagus, broccoli, corn on the cob, green beans, mushrooms, tomatoes)	390°F	6 to 10 min.
Vegetables (bell peppers, cauliflower, eggplant, onions, potatoes, zucchini)	390°F	10 to 15 min.

These times are a general guide. Foods vary in size, weight and texture—and different air fryers cook at different rates—so be sure to test your food for doneness before consuming it. For best results, some foods need to be shaken or turned during cooking.

BREAKFAST

Quick Jelly-Filled Doughnut Bites

1 package (about 7 ounces) refrigerated biscuit dough (10 biscuits)

¼ cup coarse sugar

1 cup strawberry preserves*

*If preserves are very chunky, process in food processor 10 seconds or press through fine-mesh sieve.

1 Separate biscuits. Cut each biscuit in half; roll each piece into a ball to create 20 balls.

2 Preheat air fryer to 370°F. Place sugar in shallow dish.

3 Cook doughnuts in batches 5 to 6 minutes or until golden brown. Roll warm doughnuts in sugar to coat.

4 Fill piping bag with medium star tip with preserves. Poke hole in side of each doughnut with paring knife; fill with preserves. Serve warm.

Makes 20 doughnut bites

French Toast Sticks →

4 thick slices brioche bread or challah, preferably day-old

2 eggs

⅓ cup milk

1¼ teaspoons ground cinnamon, divided

½ teaspoon vanilla

⅓ cup sugar

Maple syrup and fresh berries

1. Preheat air fryer to 350°F. Cut each bread slice into three or four 1-inch sticks. If bread is fresh, cook bread sticks 2 minutes or until slightly dry but not toasted.

2. Beat eggs, milk, ¼ teaspoon cinnamon and vanilla in shallow dish. Combine sugar and remaining 1 teaspoon cinnamon in another shallow dish.

3. Dip bread sticks quickly in egg mixture (do not let soak); roll in cinnamon-sugar to coat.

4. Line basket with parchment paper; spray with nonstick cooking spray.

5. Cook bread sticks in batches 8 minutes or until golden brown, turning halfway through cooking. Serve with maple syrup and berries.

Makes 4 servings

Breakfast Flats

1 package (about 14 ounces) refrigerated pizza dough

1½ cups (6 ounces) shredded Cheddar cheese

8 slices bacon, crisp-cooked and crumbled (optional)

4 eggs, fried

Salt and black pepper

1. Preheat air fryer to 370°F. Unroll dough on cutting board or work surface; cut into four pieces.

2. Shape each piece of dough into 6×4-inch oval. Place dough on parchment paper; top with cheese and bacon, if desired.

3. Place flatbreads with parchment paper in basket; cook in batches 4 to 6 minutes or until crusts are golden brown and cheese is melted.

4. Top warm flatbreads with fried eggs; season with salt and pepper.

Makes 4 servings

Blueberry Muffin Bread Pudding

1½ cups milk

2 eggs

4 packages (2 ounces each) mini blueberry muffins, cut into 1-inch pieces

Powdered sugar (optional)

Fresh blueberries (optional)

1 Spray four 6-ounce ramekins with nonstick cooking spray.

2 Beat milk and eggs in medium bowl until blended. Add muffins; stir to coat. Let stand 10 to 15 minutes to allow muffins to absorb milk mixture. Divide mixture among prepared ramekins.

3 Preheat air fryer to 330°F.

4 Cook 8 to 10 minutes or until lightly browned. Sprinkle with powdered sugar and serve with fresh blueberries and if desired.

Makes 4 servings

TIP

Use this recipe as a template for a variety of bread puddings—it's a great way to use up any leftover baked goods (homemade or store-bought). Try using slices of banana bread, chocolate chip muffins or cinnamon rolls instead of the blueberry muffins—simply cut them into 1-inch pieces and soak them in the milk mixture as directed.

Omelet Croissants

2 large croissants

2 eggs

¼ cup chopped mushrooms

¼ tablespoon chopped red and/or green bell pepper

Pinch salt and black pepper

¼ cup (1 ounce) shredded Cheddar cheese

1 Cut lengthwise slit across top of each croissant. Use hands to break open croissants and pull apart slightly to create space for eggs.

2 Beat eggs in medium bowl; stir in mushrooms, bell pepper, salt and black pepper. Spoon mixture into croissant openings; sprinkle with cheese.

3 Preheat air fryer to 330°F. Line basket with parchment paper.

4 Cook 12 to 15 minutes or until eggs are set and croissants are lightly browned.

Makes 2 servings

TIP

Omelet croissants can be stored in the refrigerator for up to 3 days or in the freezer for 1 month.

Quick Chocolate Chip Sticky Buns

1 package (about 11 ounces) refrigerated French bread dough

¼ cup sugar

1 teaspoon ground cinnamon

½ cup mini semisweet chocolate chips

⅓ cup chopped pecans, toasted*

2 tablespoons butter, melted

1 tablespoon maple syrup

To toast pecans, cook in preheated 325°F parchment paper-lined air fryer 3 to 4 minutes or until golden brown.

1 Unroll dough on lightly floured cutting board or work surface. Combine sugar and cinnamon in small bowl; sprinkle evenly over dough. Top with chocolate chips.

2 Starting with short side, roll up dough jelly-roll style. Cut crosswise into 12 (¾-inch) slices with serrated knife.

3 Combine pecans, butter and maple syrup in 9-inch round cake pan;* mix well. Spread in even layer; arrange dough slices cut sides up over pecan mixture.

4 Preheat air fryer to 370°F.

5 Cook buns 8 to 10 minutes or until golden brown. Invert onto serving plate; scrape any pecans or butter mixture remaining in pan over buns. Serve warm.

If 9-inch pan does not fit in your air fryer, use smaller baking dish and cook sticky buns in two batches.

Makes 12 sticky buns

Crustless Spinach Quiche

8 eggs

1 cup half-and-half

1 teaspoon Italian seasoning

¾ teaspoon salt

½ teaspoon black pepper

1 package (10 ounces) frozen chopped spinach, thawed and squeezed dry

1¼ cups (5 ounces) shredded Italian cheese blend

1 Preheat air fryer to 330°F. Line 8-inch round baking pan* with parchment paper; spray with nonstick cooking spray.

2 Beat eggs, half-and-half, Italian seasoning, salt and pepper in medium bowl until well blended. Stir in spinach and cheese; mix well. Pour into prepared pan.

3 Cook 30 minutes or until toothpick inserted into center comes out clean. Cover with foil if top is browning too quickly. Remove to wire rack; cool 10 minutes.

4 To remove quiche from pan, run knife around edge of pan to loosen. Invert quiche onto plate and remove parchment paper; invert again onto serving plate. Cut into wedges.

If 8-inch pan does not fit in your air fryer, use two smaller baking pans, reduce cooking time and cook in two batches.

Makes 6 servings

Honey-Glazed Biscuit Doughnuts

1 package (about
   16 ounces) refrigerated
   jumbo biscuit dough
   (8 biscuits)
¼ cup honey
1 teaspoon chopped
   pistachio nuts

1 Separate biscuits. Poke hole in center of each biscuit with hands or handle of wooden spoon to create doughnut shape.

2 Preheat air fryer to 370°F.

3 Cook doughnuts in batches 7 to 8 minutes or until golden brown.

4 Drizzle warm doughnuts with honey; sprinkle with pistachios. Serve immediately.

Makes 8 doughnuts

VARIATION

For cinnamon-sugar coating, combine ¼ cup sugar and 1 teaspoon ground cinnamon in shallow bowl. Dip warm doughnuts in cinnamon-sugar.

Whole Grain French Toast

1 egg
¼ cup milk
½ teaspoon ground cinnamon
¼ teaspoon ground nutmeg
8 slices whole wheat or multigrain bread
⅓ cup pure maple syrup
1 cup fresh blueberries
Powdered sugar

1 Beat egg, milk, cinnamon and nutmeg in shallow dish. Working with two slices at a time, dip bread slices in milk mixture, turning to coat both sides; let excess drip back into dish.

2 Preheat air fryer to 370°F. Spray basket with nonstick cooking spray.

3 Cook bread in batches 5 to 7 minutes or until golden brown, turning halfway through cooking.

4 Microwave maple syrup in small microwavable bowl on HIGH 30 seconds or until bubbly. Stir in blueberries. Serve French toast with blueberry mixture; sprinkle with powdered sugar.

Makes 4 servings

Air-Fried Veggie Scramble

2 large eggs

2 tablespoons milk

¼ teaspoon salt

⅛ teaspoon black pepper

2 tablespoons chopped red and/or green bell pepper

2 tablespoons chopped onion

¼ cup (1 ounce) shredded Cheddar cheese, divided

1 Spray 6×3-inch baking dish* or two small ramekins with nonstick cooking spray.

2 Beat eggs, milk, salt and black pepper in medium bowl until blended. Stir in bell pepper, onion and 2 tablespoons cheese. Pour into prepared baking dish.

3 Preheat air fryer to 350°F.

4 Cook 10 to 12 minutes or until eggs are softly set, stirring gently to break up eggs after 5 minutes. Top with remaining cheese.

*If 6-inch baking dish does not fit in your air fryer, use smaller dish or ramekins.

Makes 2 servings

TIPS

Egg scrambles are easy to customize to individual tastes—you can add or substitute different vegetables and/or meats that your family prefers. They're also a good way to use up small amounts of leftovers in your refrigerator. Serve the scrambles with toast, or use them as a filling for breakfast tacos and burritos.

Ricotta Pancakes

1 package (15 ounces) whole milk ricotta cheese

1 egg

½ teaspoon vanilla

¼ cup granulated sugar

1 cup all-purpose flour, divided

¼ teaspoon baking powder

½ cup seedless raspberry jam

Powdered sugar

Fresh raspberries (optional)

1 Beat ricotta and egg in large bowl until well blended. Stir in vanilla. Add granulated sugar, ¾ cup flour and baking powder; mix well. Place remaining ¼ cup flour in shallow dish.

2 Scoop about ¼ to ½ cup ricotta mixture into a ball. Add to dish with flour; turn to coat. Flatten into pancake about ½ inch thick; place on plate. Repeat with remaining batter. Spray pancakes with nonstick cooking spray.

3 Preheat air fryer to 370°F. Line basket with parchment paper.

4 Cook pancakes in batches 14 to 16 minutes or until lightly browned, turning and spraying with cooking spray after 10 minutes.

5 Place jam in small microwavable bowl; microwave on HIGH 30 seconds or until melted. Drizzle over warm pancakes; sprinkle with powdered sugar. Top with raspberries, if desired.

Makes 8 to 10 pancakes

Homemade Air-Fried Bagels

1 cup self-rising flour

1 cup plain Greek yogurt

1 egg, beaten

Sesame seeds, poppy
seeds, dried onion
flakes, everything bagel
seasoning (optional)

1 Combine flour and yogurt in large bowl of stand mixer.* Mix with dough hook 2 to 3 minutes or until well blended. Turn out dough onto lightly floured surface; knead 4 to 5 minutes or until dough is smooth and elastic.

2 Shape dough into a ball. Cut dough into four pieces; roll each piece into a ball. Pull and stretch dough to create round bagel shape, poking finger into centers to create holes.

3 Preheat air fryer to 330°F. Line basket with parchment paper. Place bagels on parchment; brush with egg and sprinkle with desired toppings.

4 Cook bagels 8 to 10 minutes or until lightly browned.

*Or, use heavy spatula to mix dough by hand.

Makes 4 servings

APPETIZERS

Bang Bang Cauliflower

1 head cauliflower
½ cup mayonnaise
¼ cup sweet chili sauce
1½ teaspoons hot pepper
     sauce
¼ teaspoon salt
⅛ teaspoon black pepper
¼ cup all-purpose flour
1 cup panko bread crumbs
2 green onions, chopped

1 Trim greens and stems from cauliflower. Cut into florets.

2 Combine mayonnaise, chili sauce, hot pepper sauce, salt and black pepper in shallow dish; mix well. Remove half of mixture to small bowl; set aside for serving. Place flour in another shallow dish. Place panko in third shallow dish.

3 Lightly coat cauliflower with flour. Dip in sauce mixture, turning to coat. Roll in panko to coat.

4 Preheat air fryer to 390°F. Line basket with parchment paper.

5 Cook cauliflower in batches 8 to 10 minutes or until tender and browned. Sprinkle with green onions; serve with reserved sauce.

Makes 4 to 6 servings

Pepperoni Stuffed Mushrooms

16 medium mushrooms

1 tablespoon olive oil

½ cup finely chopped onion

2 ounces pepperoni, finely chopped (about ½ cup)

¼ cup finely chopped green bell pepper

½ teaspoon seasoned salt

¼ teaspoon dried oregano

⅛ teaspoon black pepper

½ cup crushed buttery crackers (about 12)

¼ cup grated Parmesan cheese

1 tablespoon chopped fresh parsley, plus additional for garnish

1 Remove stems from mushrooms; set aside caps. Finely chop stems.

2 Heat oil in large skillet over medium-high heat. Add onion; cook and stir 2 to 3 minutes or until softened. Add mushroom stems, pepperoni, bell pepper, seasoned salt, oregano and black pepper; cook and stir 5 minutes or until vegetables are tender but not browned.

3 Remove from heat; stir in crushed crackers, cheese and 1 tablespoon parsley until blended. Spoon mixture into mushroom caps, mounding slightly in centers.

4 Preheat air fryer to 370°F. Line basket with foil; spray with nonstick cooking spray.

5 Cook mushrooms 6 to 8 minutes or until heated through. Garnish with additional parsley.

Makes 4 to 6 servings

Chicken Bacon Quesadillas

1 cup (4 ounces) shredded Colby-Jack cheese

4 (8-inch) flour tortillas

1 cup coarsely chopped cooked chicken

4 slices bacon, crisp-cooked and coarsely chopped*

½ cup pico de gallo, plus additional for serving

1 tablespoon vegetable oil

Sour cream and guacamole (optional)

Cook bacon in preheated 390°F air fryer 6 to 8 minutes or until crisp. Remove to paper towel-lined plate. Cool completely.

1 Preheat air fryer to 370°F. Spray basket with nonstick cooking spray.

2 Sprinkle ¼ cup cheese over half of one tortilla. Top with ¼ cup chicken, one fourth of bacon and 2 tablespoons pico de gallo. Fold tortilla in half over filling. Repeat with remaining ingredients. Brush both sides of quesadillas lightly with oil.

3 Cook quesadillas in batches 3 to 4 minutes or until cheese is melted and tortillas are lightly browned. Remove to cutting board; cool slightly.

4 Cut quesadillas into wedges. Serve with additional pico de gallo, sour cream and guacamole, if desired.

Makes 4 servings

Southern Crab Cakes with Rémoulade Sauce

10 ounces fresh lump crabmeat

1½ cups fresh white or sourdough bread crumbs, divided

¼ cup chopped green onions

½ cup mayonnaise, divided

1 egg white, lightly beaten

2 tablespoons coarse grain or spicy brown mustard, divided

¾ teaspoon hot pepper sauce, divided

Lemon wedges (optional)

1 Pick out and discard any shell or cartilage from crabmeat. Combine crabmeat, ¾ cup bread crumbs and green onions in medium bowl. Add ¼ cup mayonnaise, egg white, 1 tablespoon mustard and ½ teaspoon hot pepper sauce; stir gently until blended.

2 Using ¼ cup crab mixture per cake, shape into eight ½-inch-thick cakes. Place remaining ¾ cup bread crumbs in shallow dish; roll crab cakes gently in bread crumbs to coat.

3 Preheat air fryer to 370°F. Line basket with parchment paper.

4 Cook crab cakes in batches 8 to 10 minutes or until golden brown, turning halfway through cooking.

5 Meanwhile, combine remaining ¼ cup mayonnaise, 1 tablespoon mustard and ¼ teaspoon hot pepper sauce in small bowl; mix well. Serve crab cakes with sauce and lemon wedges, if desired.

Makes 8 servings

Buffalo Wings

1 cup hot pepper sauce

⅓ cup vegetable oil, plus additional for brushing

1 teaspoon sugar

½ teaspoon ground red pepper

½ teaspoon garlic powder

½ teaspoon Worcestershire sauce

⅛ teaspoon black pepper

1 pound chicken wings, tips removed, split at joints

Blue cheese or ranch dressing

Celery sticks (optional)

1 Combine hot pepper sauce, ⅓ cup oil, sugar, red pepper, garlic powder, Worcestershire sauce and black pepper in small saucepan; cook over medium heat 20 minutes. Remove from heat; pour sauce into large bowl.

2 Preheat air fryer to 370°F. Brush wings lightly with additional oil.

3 Cook wings in batches 16 to 18 minutes or until golden brown and cooked through, shaking halfway through cooking.

4 Transfer wings to bowl of sauce; stir to coat. Serve with blue cheese dressing and celery sticks, if desired.

Makes 4 servings

Spinach Florentine Flatbread

1 tablespoon olive oil

2 cloves garlic, minced

1 package (10 ounces) baby spinach

1 can (14 ounces) quartered artichoke hearts, drained and sliced

½ teaspoon salt

¼ teaspoon dried oregano

Pinch red pepper flakes

Pinch black pepper

2 rectangular pizza or flatbread crusts (about 8 ounces each)*

1 plum tomato, seeded and diced

2 cups (8 ounces) shredded Monterey Jack cheese

½ cup (2 ounces) shredded Italian cheese blend

If your air fryer is small, you may need to cut crusts in half.

1 Heat oil in large skillet over medium-high heat. Add garlic; cook and stir 30 seconds. Add half of spinach; cook and stir until slightly wilted. Add additional spinach by handfuls; cook 3 minutes or until completely wilted, stirring occasionally.

2 Remove to medium bowl; stir in artichokes, salt, oregano, red pepper flakes and black pepper.

3 Preheat air fryer to 370°F. Line basket with parchment paper.

4 Place crusts in basket. Spread spinach mixture over crusts; sprinkle with tomato, Monterey Jack and Italian cheese blend.

5 Cook flatbreads 6 to 8 minutes or until cheese is melted and edges are browned.

Makes 8 servings

TIP

For a crisper crust, cook the crusts 2 to 3 minutes before adding the topping, then continue to cook as directed above.

Empanaditas

1 tablespoon butter

1 cup finely chopped onion

2 cups finely chopped
  cooked chicken

¼ cup canned diced
  green chiles

1 tablespoon capers,
  drained and coarsely
  chopped

¼ teaspoon salt

1 cup (4 ounces) shredded
  Monterey Jack cheese

1 package (about 14 ounces)
  refrigerated pie crust
  (2 crusts)

1 egg yolk

1 teaspoon water

1 Melt butter in medium skillet over medium heat. Add onion; cook and stir 3 minutes or until softened. Add chicken, chiles, capers and salt; cook and stir 2 minute. Remove from heat; stir in cheese.

2 Roll out pie crusts to ⅛-inch thickness on lightly floured surface; cut into 2½-inch circles.

3 Place about 1 teaspoon filling in center of each circle. Fold dough in half over filling; press edges with fork to seal. Prick tops with fork to vent. Beat egg yolk and water in small bowl; brush over dough.

4 Preheat air fryer to 370°F.

5 Cook empanaditas in batches 8 to 10 minutes or until golden brown. Serve warm.

Makes about 3 dozen empanaditas

Falafel Nuggets

SAUCE

2½ cups tomato sauce

⅓ cup tomato paste

2 tablespoons lemon juice

2 teaspoons sugar

1 teaspoon onion powder

½ teaspoon salt

FALAFEL

2 cans (about 15 ounces each) chickpeas, rinsed and drained

½ cup all-purpose flour

½ cup chopped fresh parsley

1 egg

¼ cup minced onion

3 tablespoons lemon juice

2 tablespoons minced garlic

2 teaspoons ground cumin

½ teaspoon salt

¼ teaspoon ground red pepper or red pepper flakes

1 For sauce, combine tomato sauce, tomato paste, 2 tablespoons lemon juice, sugar, onion powder and ½ teaspoon salt in medium saucepan; cook over medium-low heat 20 minutes, stirring occasionally. Cover and keep warm until ready to serve.

2 For falafel, combine chickpeas, flour, parsley, egg, minced onion, 3 tablespoons lemon juice, garlic, cumin, ½ teaspoon salt and red pepper in food processor or blender; process until well blended. Shape mixture into 1-inch balls. Spray with nonstick cooking spray.

3 Preheat air fryer to 390°F. Line basket with foil; spray with cooking spray.

4 Cook falafel in batches 12 to 15 minutes or until browned, turning halfway through cooking. Serve with sauce.

Makes 12 servings

Chili Cheese Fries

1½ pounds ground beef

1 medium onion, chopped

2 cloves garlic, minced

½ cup lager

2 tablespoons chili powder

2 tablespoons tomato paste

Salt and black pepper

1 package (32 ounces) frozen French fries

1 jar (15 ounces) cheese sauce, warmed

Sour cream and chopped green onions (optional)

1 Cook beef, onion and garlic in large skillet over medium-high heat 6 to 8 minutes or until browned, stirring to break up meat. Drain fat.

2 Stir in lager, chili powder and tomato paste; mix well. Reduce heat to medium-low; cook 20 minutes or until most of liquid has evaporated, stirring occasionally. Season with salt and pepper.

3 Meanwhile, preheat air fryer to 390°F. Cook French fries 15 to 18 minutes or until browned and crisp, shaking occasionally during cooking.

4 Divide fries evenly among bowls; top with chili and cheese sauce. Garnish with sour cream and green onions.

Makes 4 to 6 servings

Mini Egg Rolls

8 ounces ground pork

3 cloves garlic, minced

1 teaspoon minced
   fresh ginger

¼ teaspoon red pepper
   flakes

6 cups (12 ounces) shredded
   coleslaw mix

¼ cup reduced-sodium
   soy sauce

1 tablespoon cornstarch

1 tablespoon seasoned
   rice vinegar

½ cup chopped green onions

28 wonton wrappers
   Sweet and sour sauce
   Chinese hot mustard

1 Combine pork, garlic, ginger and red pepper flakes in large nonstick skillet; cook and stir over medium heat about 5 minutes or until pork is cooked through, stirring to break up meat. Add coleslaw mix; cover and cook 2 minutes. Uncover; cook 2 minutes or just until coleslaw mix begins to wilt.

2 Stir soy sauce into cornstarch in small bowl until smooth and well blended; stir into pork mixture. Add vinegar; cook 2 to 3 minutes or until thickened. Remove from heat; stir in green onions.

3 Place one wonton wrapper on work surface with one corner facing you. Spoon 1 level tablespoon pork mixture across and just below center of wrapper. Fold bottom point of wrapper up over filling, then fold in sides to form envelope shape. Moisten inside edges of top point with water and roll egg roll toward top point, pressing firmly to seal. Repeat with remaining wrappers and filling. Spray egg rolls with nonstick cooking spray.

4 Preheat air fryer to 370°F. Cook egg rolls in batches, seam sides down, 3 to 5 minutes or until golden brown. Remove to wire rack; cool slightly before serving. Serve with sweet and sour sauce and mustard.

Makes 28 mini egg rolls

Potato Skins

3 small baking or red skinned potatoes, baked*

1 tablespoon butter, melted

1 teaspoon salt

⅛ teaspoon black pepper

½ cup (2 ounces) shredded Cheddar cheese

3 slices bacon, crisp-cooked and coarsely chopped (see Tip)

¼ cup sour cream

1 tablespoon snipped fresh chives

Pierce potatoes with knife; bake in 425°F oven 45 minutes, in 390°F air fryer 30 minutes or cook in microwave on HIGH 5 minutes.

1 Cut potatoes in half lengthwise. Scoop out soft centers of potatoes leaving skins intact; reserve potato flesh for another use. Brush potato skins with butter; sprinkle with salt and pepper.

2 Preheat air fryer to 370°F.

3 Cook potato skins 5 to 6 minutes or until crisp.

4 Top potato skins with cheese and bacon; cook 3 to 5 minutes or until cheese is melted. Cool slightly. Top with sour cream and chives just before serving.

Makes 3 servings

TIP

To cook bacon in the air fryer, preheat the air fryer to 390°F. Cook bacon in a single layer 6 to 8 minutes or until crisp. Drain on a paper towel-lined plate.

Pigs in a Blanket →

1 package (8 ounces) refrigerated crescent roll dough
24 cocktail franks (10- to 12-ounce package)
Mustard (optional)

1 Unroll dough on cutting board or work surface; separate into eight triangles. Cut each triangle into three long, thin triangles.

2 Place one frank on bottom (wide part) of each triangle; roll up dough toward opposite point.

3 Preheat air fryer to 350°F.

4 Cook franks in batches 3 to 4 minutes or until golden brown.

Makes 6 to 8 servings

Burger Bites

1 pound lean ground beef
2 tablespoons Dijon mustard
½ teaspoon dried minced onion
½ teaspoon salt
¼ teaspoon black pepper
Cherry tomatoes
Butter lettuce
Pickle slices
Ketchup, mustard and/or mayonnaise for dipping

1 Combine beef, mustard, minced onion, salt and pepper in medium bowl; mix gently. Shape mixture into 12 to 16 balls.

2 Preheat air fryer to 390°F. Line basket with parchment paper.

3 Cook burgers in batches 10 to 12 minutes or until cooked through (160°F). Remove to plate.

4 Thread tomatoes, lettuce, pickles and burgers onto small skewers or cocktail picks. Serve with desired dipping sauces.

Makes 6 to 8 servings

VARIATION

Add a small slice of cheese or a fresh mozzarella ball to the skewers.

Jalapeño Poppers

10 to 12 jalapeño peppers*

1 package (8 ounces)
cream cheese, softened

1½ cups (6 ounces) shredded
Cheddar cheese, divided

2 green onions, finely
chopped

½ teaspoon onion powder

¼ teaspoon salt

⅛ teaspoon garlic powder

6 slices bacon, crisp-cooked
and crumbled** or
2 tablespoons bacon
bits

2 tablespoons panko
bread crumbs

2 tablespoons grated
Parmesan or Romano
cheese

*For large jalapeño peppers,
use 10. For small peppers, use 12.*

**Cook bacon in preheated 390°F
air fryer 6 to 8 minutes or until
crisp. Remove to paper towel-
lined plate; cool completely.*

1 Cut each jalapeño pepper in half lengthwise;
remove ribs and seeds.

2 Combine cream cheese, 1 cup Cheddar, green
onions, onion powder, salt and garlic powder
in medium bowl; mix well. Stir in bacon.

3 Fill each pepper half with about 1 tablespoon
cheese mixture; sprinkle with remaining ½ cup
Cheddar, panko and Parmesan.

4 Preheat air fryer to 370°F. Line basket with
parchment paper or foil.

5 Cook filled peppers in batches 5 to 7 minutes
or until cheese is melted and browned but
peppers are still firm.

Makes 20 to 24 poppers

Fried Macaroni and Cheese Bites

4 ounces uncooked
   elbow macaroni

1 tablespoon butter

1 tablespoon all-purpose
   flour

1 cup milk

½ teaspoon salt, divided

1 cup (4 ounces) shredded
   Cheddar cheese

½ cup (2 ounces) shredded
   Swiss cheese

½ cup (2 ounces) shredded
   smoked Gouda cheese

2 eggs

2 tablespoons water

1 cup plain dry bread
   crumbs

½ teaspoon Italian seasoning
   Marinara sauce, warmed

1 Cook macaroni in large saucepan of boiling salted water 7 minutes or until al dente. Drain and set aside.

2 Melt butter in same saucepan over medium-high heat. Whisk in flour until smooth. Cook 1 minute, whisking frequently. Add milk in thin, steady stream; cook about 8 minutes or until sauce thickens, whisking frequently. Add ¼ teaspoon salt. Gradually stir in cheeses until melted and smooth. Stir in macaroni.

3 Spray 9-inch square baking pan with nonstick cooking spray. Spread macaroni and cheese in prepared pan; smooth top. Cover with plastic wrap; refrigerate 4 hours or until firm and cold.

4 Turn out macaroni and cheese onto cutting board; cut into 1-inch pieces. Preheat air fryer to 370°F.

5 Beat eggs and 2 tablespoons water in shallow dish. Combine bread crumbs, Italian seasoning and remaining ¼ teaspoon salt in another shallow dish. Working with a few pieces at a time, dip macaroni and cheese pieces in egg, then roll in bread crumb mixture to coat. Place on baking sheet.

6 Cook in batches 3 minutes or until golden brown, turning halfway through cooking. Serve with marinara sauce.

Makes about 4 servings

Bruschetta

4 plum tomatoes, seeded and diced

½ cup packed fresh basil leaves, finely chopped

5 tablespoons olive oil, divided

2 cloves garlic, minced

2 teaspoons finely chopped oil-packed sun-dried tomatoes

¼ teaspoon salt

⅛ teaspoon black pepper

16 slices Italian bread

2 tablespoons grated Parmesan cheese

1 Combine fresh tomatoes, basil, 3 tablespoons oil, garlic, sun-dried tomatoes, salt and pepper in large bowl; mix well. Let stand at room temperature 1 hour to blend flavors.

2 Brush remaining 2 tablespoons oil over one side of bread slices; sprinkle with cheese.

3 Preheat air fryer to 350°F. Cook bread slices in single layer 3 to 5 minutes or until toasted.

4 Top each bread slice with 1 tablespoon tomato mixture.

Makes 8 servings

Spicy Korean Chicken Wings

3 tablespoons peanut oil, divided

2 tablespoons grated fresh ginger

½ cup soy sauce

¼ cup cider vinegar

¼ cup honey

¼ cup chili garlic sauce

2 tablespoons orange juice

1 tablespoon dark sesame oil

18 chicken wings or drummettes

Sesame seeds (optional)

1 Heat 2 tablespoons peanut oil in large saucepan over medium-high heat. Add ginger; cook and stir 1 minute. Add soy sauce, vinegar, honey, chili garlic sauce, orange juice and sesame oil; cook and stir 2 minutes.

2 Pat wings dry with paper towels; remove and discard wing tips. Brush with remaining 1 tablespoon peanut oil.

3 Preheat air fryer to 370°F. Spray basket with nonstick cooking spray.

4 Cook wings in batches 16 to 18 minutes or until browned and cooked through, shaking occasionally during cooking. Remove to paper towel-lined plate.

5 Add wings to saucepan; stir to coat with sauce. Sprinkle with sesame seeds, if desired.

Makes 6 to 8 servings

Spinach-Artichoke Dip

1 package (8 ounces)
  baby spinach

1 package (8 ounces)
  cream cheese, softened

¼ cup mayonnaise

1 clove garlic, minced

1 teaspoon dried basil

½ teaspoon dried thyme

¼ teaspoon salt

¼ teaspoon red pepper
  flakes

¼ teaspoon black pepper

1 can (about 14 ounces)
  artichoke hearts,
  drained and chopped

¾ cup grated Parmesan
  cheese, divided

  Toasted French bread
  slices or tortilla chips

1 Spray 1-quart shallow baking dish that fits inside air fryer with nonstick cooking spray.

2 Place spinach in large microwavable bowl; cover and microwave on HIGH 2 minutes or until wilted. Uncover; let stand until cool enough to handle. Squeeze dry and coarsely chop.

3 Whisk cream cheese, mayonnaise, garlic, basil, thyme, salt, red pepper flakes and black pepper in medium bowl until well blended. Stir in spinach, artichokes and ½ cup Parmesan. Spread in prepared baking dish; sprinkle with remaining ¼ cup Parmesan.

4 Preheat air fryer to 330°F. Cook about 20 minutes or until edges are golden brown. Cool slightly; serve warm with toasted bread slices.

Makes 6 to 8 servings

Crispy Mushrooms

MUSHROOMS

- ½ cup all-purpose flour
- ½ cup garlic and herb-flavored bread crumbs
- ½ cup grated Parmesan cheese
- ½ teaspoon paprika
- ½ teaspoon salt
- ¼ teaspoon black pepper
- 2 eggs
- 1 teaspoon water
- 1 package (8 ounces) whole mushrooms

GARLIC MAYONNAISE

- ½ cup mayonnaise
- 2 teaspoons minced garlic
- 1 teaspoon lemon juice
- Chopped fresh parsley (optional)

1 Combine flour, bread crumbs, cheese, paprika, salt and pepper in shallow dish. Beat eggs and water in another shallow dish.

2 Use fork to dip mushrooms into egg mixture, allowing excess to drip back into dish. Roll in bread crumb mixture to coat completely. Spray mushrooms with nonstick cooking spray.

3 Preheat air fryer to 370°F. Line basket with parchment paper.

4 Cook mushrooms in batches 6 to 8 minutes or until golden brown, shaking and spraying with cooking spray halfway through cooking.

5 Meanwhile, combine mayonnaise, garlic and lemon juice in small bowl; mix well. Sprinkle with parsley, if desired. Serve with mushrooms.

Makes 4 servings

SNACKS

Bagel Chips with Everything Seasoning Dip

2 large bagels, cut vertically into thin (¼-inch) slices

1 container (12 ounces) whipped cream cheese

1½ tablespoons minced green onion (green part only)

1 teaspoon dried minced onion

1 teaspoon granulated garlic

1 teaspoon sesame seeds

1 teaspoon poppy seeds

¼ teaspoon coarse salt

1 Preheat air fryer to 350°F.

2 Coat bagel slices generously with butter-flavored nonstick cooking spray.

3 Cook bagel slices in batches 7 to 8 minutes or until golden brown, shaking occasionally during cooking.

4 Meanwhile, combine cream cheese, green onion, minced onion, garlic, sesame seeds, poppy seeds and salt in medium bowl; mix well. Serve with bagel chips.

Makes about 8 servings

Tasty Turkey Turnovers

1 package (about 8 ounces) refrigerated crescent roll dough sheet

2 tablespoons honey mustard, plus additional for serving

3 ounces thinly sliced deli turkey

¾ cup broccoli coleslaw mix

1 egg white, beaten

1 Unroll dough on lightly floured surface. Use cookie cutter or drinking glass to cut out six 3½-inch circles.

2 Brush 2 tablespoons honey mustard lightly over dough; top with turkey and coleslaw mix. Brush edges of dough with egg white. Fold dough in half over filling; press edges with fork to seal. Brush tops with egg white.

3 Preheat air fryer to 370°F. Spray basket with nonstick cooking spray.

4 Cook turnovers in batches 6 to 7 minutes or until golden brown. Let stand 5 minutes before serving. Serve warm or at room temperature with additional honey mustard, if desired.

Makes 6 servings

Roasted Chickpeas →

1 can (about 15 ounces) chickpeas, rinsed, drained and patted dry
2 tablespoons olive oil
½ teaspoon salt
½ teaspoon black pepper
1½ teaspoons chili powder
¼ to ½ teaspoon ground red pepper
1 lime, cut into wedges (optional)

1 Combine chickpeas, oil, salt and black pepper in medium bowl; mix well.

2 Preheat air fryer to 390°F.

3 Cook chickpeas 8 to 10 minutes or until beginning to brown, shaking occasionally during cooking.

4 Return to medium bowl. Sprinkle with chili powder and red pepper; toss to coat. Serve with lime wedges, if desired.

Makes about 4 servings

NOTE

Roasted chickpeas are great as a snack, or use them as a topping for salads—chickpeas offer a delicious crunch and a healthier alternative to croutons.

Herbed Potato Chips

1 tablespoon minced fresh dill, thyme or rosemary leaves *or* 1 teaspoon dried dill weed, thyme or rosemary
¼ teaspoon garlic salt
⅛ teaspoon black pepper
2 medium red potatoes

1 Combine dill, garlic salt and pepper in small bowl; mix well.

2 Cut potatoes crosswise into very thin slices (about 1⁄16 inch). Pat dry with paper towels. Spray potatoes with nonstick cooking spray; sprinkle with seasoning mixture.

3 Preheat air fryer to 390°F. Line basket with parchment paper; spray with cooking spray.

4 Cook potatoes 10 to 12 minutes or until golden brown, shaking and spraying with cooking spray halfway through cooking.

Makes 2 servings

Crunchy Parmesan Zucchini Sticks

1 package (3 ounces) ramen
  noodles, any flavor
½ cup shredded Parmesan
  cheese
½ cup all-purpose flour
1 egg
1 tablespoon water
3 medium zucchini, cut
  into 3-inch sticks
  Marinara sauce, warmed

1 Combine noodles and cheese in food processor; pulse until fine crumbs form. Pour into shallow dish.

2 Combine flour and ramen seasoning packet in another shallow dish. Beat egg and water in third shallow dish.

3 Dip zucchini sticks in flour mixture, then in egg, allowing excess to drip back into dish. Roll in noodle mixture to coat. Spray with nonstick cooking spray.

4 Preheat air fryer to 390°F. Line basket with parchment paper; spray with cooking spray.

5 Cook zucchini in batches 8 to 10 minutes or until tender and golden brown, shaking halfway through cooking. Serve warm with marinara sauce.

Makes 6 servings

Butternut Squash Chips

Lime Yogurt Dip
(recipe follows)
1 butternut squash (about
2½ pounds), peeled
and seeded
½ teaspoon garlic powder
¼ teaspoon salt
¼ teaspoon ground
red pepper
2 teaspoons vegetable oil

1 Prepare Lime Yogurt Dip.

2 Cut squash in half lengthwise, then cut crosswise into thin slices. Place squash in large bowl. Preheat air fryer to 390°F.

3 Combine garlic powder, salt and red pepper in small bowl; mix well. Drizzle squash with oil; sprinkle with seasoning mix and toss gently to coat.

4 Cook squash 15 to 18 minutes or until browned and crisp, shaking occasionally during cooking. Serve with dip.

Makes 4 servings

LIME YOGURT DIP

Combine ¼ cup mayonnaise, ¼ cup plain Greek yogurt, 1 teaspoon lime juice and ¼ teaspoon grated lime peel in small bowl. Refrigerate until ready to serve.

Pepperoni Pizza Rounds →

1 package (12 ounces) refrigerated flaky buttermilk biscuits (10 biscuits)

1 package (5 ounces) mini pepperoni slices

¼ cup chopped bell pepper (optional)

1 tablespoon dried basil

½ cup pizza sauce

1½ cups (6 ounces) shredded mozzarella cheese

Shredded Parmesan cheese (optional)

1 Spray 20 (2½-inch) silicone muffin cups with nonstick cooking spray.

2 Separate biscuits; split each biscuit in half horizontally to create 20 rounds. Place in prepared muffin cups. Press four pepperoni slices into center of each round. Sprinkle with bell pepper, if desired, and basil. Top with pizza sauce; sprinkle with mozzarella.

3 Preheat air fryer to 370°F.

4 Cook pizzas in batches 14 to 16 minutes or until golden brown. Sprinkle with Parmesan, if desired. Cool in cups 2 minutes; remove to wire racks. Serve warm.

Makes 20 mini pizzas

Garlic-Herb Parmesan Dipping Sticks

1 package (about 14 ounces) refrigerated pizza dough

¾ cup garlic and herb spreadable cheese

¾ cup (3 ounces) shredded Italian cheese blend

¼ cup grated Parmesan cheese

½ teaspoon dried oregano

Marinara sauce and/or ranch dressing (optional)

1 Roll out dough into 12-inch square on lightly floured surface. Spread garlic and herb cheese evenly over dough; top with Italian cheese blend, Parmesan and oregano. Cut dough in half or thirds to fit into basket.

2 Preheat air fryer to 390°F. Line basket with parchment paper; spray with nonstick cooking spray.

3 Cook dough in batches 6 to 8 minutes or until golden brown. Cool on wire rack 5 minutes.

4 Cut lengthwise into strips. Serve with marinara sauce, if desired.

Makes 12 servings

Savory Pita Chips

2 whole wheat or white
    pita bread rounds
2 tablespoons grated
    Parmesan cheese
1 teaspoon dried basil
¼ teaspoon garlic powder

1 Cut pita breads in half horizontally; split into two rounds. Cut each round into six wedges; spray wedges with nonstick cooking spray.

2 Combine cheese, basil and garlic powder in small bowl; mix well. Sprinkle over pita wedges.

3 Preheat air fryer to 350°F.

4 Cook pita wedges 8 to 10 minutes or until golden brown, shaking occasionally during cooking. Cool completely.

Makes 4 servings

CINNAMON CRISPS

Substitute butter-flavored cooking spray for nonstick cooking spray and 1 tablespoon sugar mixed with ¼ teaspoon ground cinnamon for Parmesan, basil and garlic powder.

Air-Fried Bowtie Bites →

8 ounces uncooked bowtie (farfalle) pasta or favorite shaped pasta (such as shells or tubes)

1½ tablespoons olive oil

¼ cup grated Parmesan cheese

½ teaspoon salt

½ teaspoon garlic powder

¼ teaspoon black pepper

Marinara sauce, warmed (optional)

1 Prepare pasta according to package directions until al dente. Drain pasta (do not rinse); transfer to large bowl.

2 Preheat air fryer to 390°F.

3 Drizzle pasta with oil. Add cheese, salt, garlic powder and pepper; toss to coat.

4 Cook pasta in single layer 10 to 12 minutes or until lightly browned and crisp around edges, shaking occasionally during cooking. Season with additional salt and pepper. Serve with marinara sauce, if desired.

Makes 8 to 10 servings

Cinnamon-Sugar Sweet Potato Fries

1 medium sweet potato

1 tablespoon sugar

½ teaspoon ground cinnamon

1 teaspoon butter, melted

1 Preheat air fryer to 390°F. Peel sweet potato; cut into thin strips. Spray with nonstick cooking spray.

2 Cook sweet potato strips in single layer 15 to 18 minutes or until lightly browned, shaking occasionally during cooking. Remove to medium bowl.

3 Combine sugar and cinnamon in small bowl; mix well.

4 Drizzle hot sweet potato with butter; sprinkle with cinnamon-sugar and toss to coat. Serve immediately.

Makes 2 servings

Garlic Roasted Olives and Tomatoes →

1 cup assorted olives, pitted

1 cup grape tomatoes, halved

4 cloves garlic, sliced

1 tablespoon olive oil

1 tablespoon herbes de Provence

1 Pat olives dry with paper towels.

2 Combine olives, tomatoes, garlic and oil in medium bowl. Stir in herbes de Provence; mix well.

3 Preheat air fryer to 370°F. Spread olive mixture in basket.

4 Cook 5 to 7 minutes or until tomatoes are browned and blistered, shaking occasionally during cooking.

Makes about 2 cups

SERVING SUGGESTION

Serve as an appetizer with toasted bread, or toss with hot cooked pasta as a main dish.

Kale Chips

1 large bunch kale (about 1 pound)

1 tablespoon olive oil

1 teaspoon garlic powder

½ teaspoon salt

½ teaspoon black pepper

1 Wash kale; pat dry with paper towels. Remove and discard center ribs and stems. Cut leaves crosswise into 2- to 3-inch-wide pieces.

2 Combine kale, oil, garlic powder, salt and pepper in large bowl; toss to coat.

3 Preheat air fryer to 390°F.

4 Cook kale in batches 3 to 4 minutes or until edges are lightly browned and leaves are crisp, shaking halfway through cooking. Cool completely.

Makes 6 servings

Pita Cheese Straws →

3 (6-inch) pita bread rounds
2 tablespoons butter, melted
1 clove garlic, minced
1 teaspoon Italian seasoning
¾ teaspoon salt
¼ cup grated Parmesan cheese
   French onion dip (optional)

1 Cut pita bread in half horizontally; split into two rounds. Combine butter, garlic and Italian seasoning in small bowl; mix well.

2 Brush tops of pitas with butter mixture; sprinkle with salt and cheese. Cut into ½-inch strips with pizza cutter.

3 Preheat air fryer to 330°F.

4 Cook pita strips in single layer 6 to 8 minutes or until edges are golden brown. Serve with dip, if desired.

Makes 6 servings

Sugar and Spice Twists

2 tablespoons granulated sugar
½ teaspoon ground cinnamon
1 package (about 11 ounces) refrigerated breadstick dough (12 breadsticks)

1 Combine sugar and cinnamon in shallow dish; mix well.

2 Separate breadsticks; roll each piece into 12-inch rope. Roll ropes in cinnamon-sugar to coat. Twist each rope into pretzel shape.

3 Preheat air fryer to 370°F. Line basket with parchment paper; spray with nonstick cooking spray.

4 Cook pretzel twists in batches 8 to 10 minutes or until lightly browned. Remove to wire rack to cool 5 minutes. Serve warm.

Makes 12 servings

SANDWICHES & WRAPS

Bacon-Tomato Grilled Cheese

4 slices bacon, cut in half

4 slices whole wheat or
   white bread

2 slices sharp Cheddar
   cheese

2 slices Gouda cheese

2 slices tomato

1 Preheat air fryer to 400°F. Cook bacon 6 to 8 minutes or until crisp; remove to paper towel-lined plate. *Reduce temperature of air fryer to 350°F.*

2 Place two bread slices on plate. Top each with one slice Cheddar, one slice Gouda, one slice tomato, two slices bacon and remaining bread slice.

3 Cook sandwiches 3 to 5 minutes or until cheese is melted and bread is golden brown.

Makes 2 servings

Chicken Parmesan Sliders

4 boneless skinless chicken breasts (4 to 6 ounces each)

¼ cup all-purpose flour

2 eggs

1 tablespoon water

1 cup Italian-seasoned dry bread crumbs

½ cup grated Parmesan cheese

Salt and black pepper

12 slider buns (about 3 inches), split

¾ cup marinara sauce

6 tablespoons Alfredo sauce

6 slices (1 ounce each) mozzarella cheese, cut into halves

6 tablespoons prepared pesto

2 tablespoons butter, melted

¼ teaspoon garlic powder

1 Pound chicken to ½-inch thickness between two sheets of waxed paper or plastic wrap with rolling pin or meat mallet. Cut each chicken breast crosswise into three pieces about the size of slider buns.

2 Place flour in shallow dish. Beat eggs and water in second shallow dish. Combine bread crumbs and Parmesan in third shallow dish. Season flour and egg mixtures with pinch of salt and pepper. Coat chicken lightly with flour, then dip in egg mixture, allowing excess to drip back into dish. Roll in bread crumb mixture to coat. Place on baking sheet; let stand 10 minutes.

3 Preheat air fryer to 370°F. Line basket with foil.

4 Cook chicken in batches 10 to 12 minutes or until golden brown and no longer pink in center, turning halfway through cooking. Remove to plate.

5 Working in batches, arrange bottom halves of slider buns cut sides up in foil-lined basket. Spread 1 tablespoon marinara sauce over each bottom bun; top with piece of chicken. Spread ½ tablespoon Alfredo sauce over chicken; top with half slice of mozzarella. Spread ½ tablespoon pesto over cheese; cover with top halves of buns.

6 Combine butter and garlic powder in small bowl; brush mixture over buns. Cook sliders 1 to 2 minutes or until cheese is melted and buns are lightly browned.

Makes 12 sliders

Barbecue Cauliflower Calzones

1 head cauliflower, cut into florets and thinly sliced

2 tablespoons olive oil

Salt and black pepper

¾ cup barbecue sauce, plus additional for serving

1 container (about 14 ounces) refrigerated pizza dough

½ onion, chopped

1 cup (4 ounces) shredded mozzarella cheese

Ranch or blue cheese dressing (optional)

1 Preheat air fryer to 390°F.

2 Place cauliflower in medium bowl; drizzle with oil. Season with salt and pepper; toss to coat.

3 Cook cauliflower 6 to 8 minutes or until slightly tender and lightly browned, shaking halfway through cooking. Return to medium bowl; stir in ¾ cup barbecue sauce. *Reduce temperature of air fryer to 370°F.*

4 Unroll dough onto lightly floured cutting board or work surface. Stretch dough into 11×17-inch rectangle; cut into quarters. Place one fourth of onion on half of each piece of dough. Top with one fourth of cauliflower and ¼ cup cheese. Fold dough over filling; roll and pinch edges to seal. Spray with nonstick cooking spray.

5 Cook calzone in batches 5 to 7 minutes or until golden brown. Serve with additional barbecue sauce and ranch dressing, if desired.

Makes 4 servings

Chicken Fajita Roll-Ups

1 cup ranch dressing

1 teaspoon chili powder

1 tablespoon vegetable oil

2 teaspoons lime juice

2 teaspoons fajita seasoning mix

½ teaspoon chipotle chili powder

¼ teaspoon salt

4 boneless skinless chicken breasts (4 to 6 ounces each)

4 fajita-size flour tortillas (8 to 9 inches), warmed

1 cup (4 ounces) shredded Cheddar cheese

1 cup (4 ounces) shredded Monterey Jack cheese

3 cups shredded lettuce

1 cup pico de gallo

1 Combine ranch dressing and chili powder in small bowl; mix well. Refrigerate until ready to serve.

2 Combine oil, lime juice, fajita seasoning mix, chipotle chili powder and salt in small bowl; mix well. Coat both sides of chicken with spice mixture.

3 Preheat air fryer to 370°F. Cook chicken 14 to 18 minutes or until no longer pink in center. Remove to plate; let stand 5 minutes before slicing. Cut chicken breasts in half lengthwise, then cut crosswise into ½-inch strips.

4 Sprinkle each tortilla with ¼ cup Cheddar and ¼ cup Monterey Jack. Cook in batches 1 to 2 minutes or until cheese is melted. Remove tortilla to clean work surface or cutting board.

5 Sprinkle ¾ cup shredded lettuce down center of each tortilla; top with ¼ cup pico de gallo and one fourth of chicken. Roll up to enclose filling. Cut in half diagonally; serve with ranch dipping sauce.

Makes 4 servings

Greek-Style Steak Sandwiches →

2 teaspoons Greek
    seasoning or dried
    oregano
1 beef flank steak
    (about 1½ pounds)
4 pita bread rounds, cut
    in half crosswise
1 small cucumber,
    thinly sliced
1 tomato, cut into
    thin wedges
½ cup sliced red onion
½ cup crumbled feta cheese
¼ cup red wine vinaigrette
1 cup plain yogurt

1 Rub Greek seasoning over both sides of steak. Place on plate; cover and refrigerate 30 to 60 minutes.

2 Preheat air fryer to 400°F. Cook steak 6 minutes; turn and cook about 6 minutes for medium rare. Remove to cutting board; tent with foil. Let stand 10 minutes before slicing.

3 Slice steak into thin strips against the grain. Divide meat among pita halves; top with cucumber, tomato, onion and cheese. Drizzle with vinaigrette; serve with yogurt.

Makes 4 to 6 servings

Classic Grilled Cheese

4 slices white bread
4 slices American cheese
2 tablespoons butter,
    melted

1 Place two bread slices on plate. Top each with two slices cheese and remaining bread slices. Brush outsides of sandwiches with butter.

2 Preheat air fryer to 350°F.

3 Cook sandwiches 6 to 8 minutes or until cheese is melted and bread is golden brown, turning halfway through cooking.

Makes 2 servings

Tuscan Portobello Melt

1 portobello mushroom cap,
   thinly sliced

½ small red onion,
   thinly sliced

½ cup grape tomatoes

1 tablespoon olive oil

1 teaspoon balsamic vinegar

⅛ teaspoon salt

⅛ teaspoon dried thyme

⅛ teaspoon black pepper

4 slices sourdough bread

2 slices provolone cheese

2 teaspoons Dijon mustard

2 slices Monterey Jack
   cheese

2 tablespoons butter,
   melted

1 Combine mushroom, onion and tomatoes in medium bowl; drizzle with oil and vinegar. Sprinkle with salt, thyme and pepper; toss to coat.

2 Preheat air fryer to 390°F. Spray basket with nonstick cooking spray.

3 Cook vegetables 8 to 10 minutes or until tender, shaking halfway through cooking.

4 Place two bread slices on plate. Top each with one slice provolone; spread mustard over cheese. Top with half of vegetables, one slice Monterey Jack and remaining bread slice. Brush outsides of sandwiches with butter.

5 Cook sandwiches 3 to 5 minutes or until cheese is melted and bread is golden brown.

Makes 2 servings

Buffalo Chicken Wraps

2 boneless skinless chicken breasts (about 4 ounces each)

4 tablespoons buffalo wing sauce, divided

1 cup broccoli coleslaw mix

1 tablespoon blue cheese dressing

2 (8-inch) whole wheat tortillas, warmed

1 Place chicken in large resealable food storage bag. Add 2 tablespoons buffalo sauce; seal bag and turn to coat. Marinate in refrigerator 15 minutes.

2 Preheat air fryer to 370°F. Cook chicken 14 to 18 minutes or until no longer pink in center.

3 When cool enough to handle, slice chicken; combine with remaining 2 tablespoons buffalo sauce in medium bowl.

4 Combine coleslaw mix and blue cheese dressing in small bowl; mix well. Spoon chicken and coleslaw down center of tortillas; roll up to enclose filling. Cut in half diagonally.

Makes 2 servings

TIP

If you don't like the spicy flavor of buffalo wing sauce, substitute your favorite barbecue sauce.

Pizza Sandwich →

1 loaf (12 ounces) focaccia
½ cup pizza sauce
20 slices pepperoni
8 slices (1 ounce each) mozzarella cheese
1 can (2¼ ounces) sliced mushrooms, drained
 Red pepper flakes (optional)

1 Cut focaccia in half horizontally.* Spread cut sides of both halves with pizza sauce. Layer bottom half with pepperoni, cheese and mushrooms; sprinkle with red pepper flakes, if desired. Cover with top half of focaccia.

2 Preheat air fryer to 370°F.

3 Cook sandwich 3 to 5 minutes or until cheese is melted and bread is golden brown. Cut into wedges.

Depending on the size of your air fryer, you may need to cut the focaccia in half vertically to fit.

Makes 4 to 6 servings

Bacon Burgers

8 slices bacon, crisp-cooked, divided
2 pounds ground beef
1½ teaspoons chopped fresh thyme *or* ½ teaspoon dried thyme
½ teaspoon salt
⅛ teaspoon black pepper
4 slices Swiss cheese
4 hamburger buns or rolls, split

1 Crumble four slices bacon.

2 Combine beef, crumbled bacon, thyme, salt and pepper in medium bowl; mix gently. Shape mixture into four patties.

3 Preheat air fryer to 370°F. Line basket with foil.

4 Cook patties 12 to 14 minutes or until cooked through (160°F) or to desired doneness, turning halfway through cooking. Top with cheese during last 2 minutes of cooking. Serve burgers on buns with remaining bacon slices.

Makes 4 servings

Nashville-Style Hot Chicken Sandwiches

2 tablespoons hot pepper sauce, divided

2 tablespoons dill pickle juice, divided

1 teaspoon salt, divided

2 pounds chicken breast strips or tenders

1 cup all-purpose flour

½ teaspoon black pepper

1 egg

½ cup buttermilk

¼ cup olive oil

1 tablespoon red pepper flakes

1 tablespoon packed brown sugar

½ teaspoon paprika

½ teaspoon chili powder

¼ teaspoon garlic powder

4 to 6 brioche buns, toasted

White Cheddar cheese slices (optional)

Coleslaw and dill pickle slices

1 Combine 1 tablespoon hot pepper sauce, 1 tablespoon pickle juice and ½ teaspoon salt in large resealable food storage bag. Add chicken; seal bag and turn to coat. Refrigerate at least 1 hour or overnight.

2 Combine flour, remaining ½ teaspoon salt and black pepper in shallow dish. Beat egg, buttermilk, remaining 1 tablespoon hot pepper sauce and 1 tablespoon pickle juice in another shallow dish. Remove chicken from marinade; discard marinade. Coat chicken with flour mixture, then dip in egg mixture, allowing excess to drip back into dish. Roll in flour mixture again to coat. Spray with nonstick cooking spray.

3 Preheat air fryer to 390°F. Spray basket with nonstick cooking spray. Cook chicken in batches 14 to 18 minutes or until no longer pink in center, turning halfway through cooking and spraying again with cooking spray. Remove chicken to medium bowl.

4 Whisk oil, red pepper flakes, brown sugar, paprika, chili powder and garlic powder in small bowl until blended. Pour over chicken; turn to coat.

5 Serve chicken on toasted buns with cheese, if desired, coleslaw and pickles.

Makes 4 to 6 servings

Turkey Dinner Quesadillas →

4 (10- to 12-inch) flour
    tortillas
8 slices deli turkey
8 slices (1 ounce each)
    Swiss cheese
½ cup whole berry
    cranberry sauce
1 cup baby spinach

1 Place tortillas on work surface. Cut one slit from outer edge of each tortilla to center.

2 Arrange two turkey slices, two cheese slices, 2 tablespoons cranberry sauce and ¼ cup spinach in each of four quadrants of tortillas. Beginning with cut edge, fold each tortilla into quarters, covering each quadrant until entire tortilla is folded into one large triangle.

3 Preheat air fryer to 370°F. Spray outside of quesadillas with nonstick cooking spray.

4 Cook quesadillas in batches 3 to 5 minutes or until lightly browned.

Makes 4 servings

Spinach and Roasted Pepper Panini

1 loaf (12 ounces) focaccia
1½ cups fresh spinach leaves
1 jar (about 7 ounces)
    roasted red peppers,
    drained
4 ounces fontina cheese,
    thinly sliced
½ cup thinly sliced red onion

1 Cut focaccia in half horizontally. Layer bottom half with spinach, roasted peppers, cheese and onion. Cover with top half of focaccia. Cut into six wedges.

2 Preheat air fryer to 370°F. Line basket with parchment paper.

3 Cook panini in batches 3 to 5 minutes or until cheese is melted and bread is golden brown.

Makes 6 servings

MAIN DISHES

Buttermilk Air-Fried Chicken

1 cut-up whole chicken
  (about 3 pounds)
1 cup buttermilk
¾ cup all-purpose flour
½ teaspoon salt
½ teaspoon ground
  red pepper
¼ teaspoon garlic powder
2 cups plain dry bread
  crumbs

1 Place chicken pieces in large resealable food storage bag. Pour buttermilk over chicken; seal bag and turn to coat. Marinate in refrigerator at least 2 hours.

2 Combine flour, salt, red pepper and garlic powder in large shallow dish. Place bread crumbs in another shallow dish.

3 Preheat air fryer to 370°F. Spray basket with nonstick cooking spray.

4 Working with one piece at a time, remove chicken from bag. (Discard buttermilk.) Coat chicken with flour mixture, then roll in bread crumbs to coat. Spray with cooking spray.

5 Cook chicken in batches 20 to 25 minutes or until browned, crisp and cooked through (165°F).

Makes 4 servings

Air-Fried Beef Taquitos

12 ounces ground beef

¼ cup chopped onion

1 tablespoon taco
   seasoning mix

6 corn tortillas

⅓ cup shredded Cheddar
   cheese, plus additional
   for topping

   Salsa, sour cream and
   guacamole (optional)

1 Cook beef and onion in large skillet over medium-high heat 6 to 8 minutes or until browned, stirring to break up meat. Drain fat. Stir in taco seasoning mix; cook 2 minutes.

2 Spoon about 2 tablespoons beef mixture down center of each tortilla; top with 1 tablespoon cheese. Roll up tortillas to enclose filling; secure with toothpicks. Spray with nonstick cooking spray.

3 Preheat air fryer to 370°F.

4 Cook taquitos in single layer 3 to 4 minutes or until tortillas are browned and crisp. Remove toothpicks before serving; top with salsa, sour cream, guacamole and/or additional cheese, if desired.

Makes 6 servings

VARIATION

Substitute ground turkey or pork for the ground beef in the taquito filling, or use leftover chopped cooked chicken or pork.

Parmesan-Crusted Tilapia

⅔ cup plus 2 tablespoons grated Parmesan cheese, divided

⅔ cup panko bread crumbs

⅓ cup prepared Alfredo sauce (refrigerated or jarred)

1½ teaspoons dried parsley flakes

6 tilapia fillets (6 ounces each)

Shaved Parmesan cheese (optional)

Minced fresh parsley (optional)

1 Combine ⅔ cup grated cheese and panko in medium bowl; mix well. Combine Alfredo sauce, remaining 2 tablespoons grated cheese and parsley flakes in small bowl; mix well.

2 Spread Alfredo sauce mixture over top of fish, coating in thick even layer. Top with panko mixture, pressing gently to adhere.

3 Preheat air fryer to 390°F. Line basket with foil or parchment paper; spray with nonstick cooking spray.

4 Cook fish in batches 8 to 10 minutes or until crust is golden brown and fish begins to flake when tested with fork. Garnish with shaved cheese and fresh parsley.

Makes 6 servings

Garlic Chicken with Roasted Vegetables

3 tablespoons olive oil, divided

1 teaspoon salt

1 teaspoon dried oregano

1 teaspoon paprika

½ teaspoon black pepper

2 cloves garlic, minced

4 boneless skinless chicken breasts (4 to 6 ounces each)

2 cups Brussels sprouts, trimmed and halved

2 small yellow onions, cut into wedges

1 cup frozen crinkle-cut carrots

Salt and black pepper

1 Combine 2 tablespoons oil, 1 teaspoon salt, oregano, paprika, ½ teaspoon pepper and garlic in small bowl; mix well. Brush over chicken.

2 Preheat air fryer to 370°F. Line basket with parchment paper.

3 Cook chicken in single layer 15 to 20 minutes or until browned and no longer pink in center. Remove to plate; tent with foil to keep warm. *Increase temperature of air fryer to 390°F.*

4 Combine Brussels sprouts, onions, carrots and remaining 1 tablespoon oil in medium bowl; toss to coat. Season with salt and pepper.

5 Cook vegetables in batches 6 to 8 minutes or until tender and lightly browned, shaking halfway through cooking.

Makes 4 servings

Cauliflower Tacos with Chipotle Crema

1 package (8 ounces) sliced cremini mushrooms

4 tablespoons olive oil, divided

1¾ teaspoons salt, divided

1 head cauliflower, cut into 1-inch florets

1 teaspoon ground cumin

½ teaspoon dried oregano

¼ teaspoon ground coriander

¼ teaspoon ground cinnamon

¼ teaspoon black pepper

½ cup sour cream

2 teaspoons lime juice

½ teaspoon chipotle chili powder

½ cup vegetarian refried beans

8 (6-inch) corn or flour tortillas

Chopped fresh cilantro

Pickled Red Onions (recipe follows) or chopped red onion (optional)

1 Combine mushrooms, 1 tablespoon oil and ¼ teaspoon salt in medium bowl; toss to coat.

2 Place cauliflower in large bowl. Add remaining 3 tablespoons oil, 1 teaspoon salt, cumin, oregano, coriander, cinnamon and pepper; toss to coat.

3 Preheat air fryer to 390°F. Spray basket with nonstick cooking spray. Cook cauliflower in batches 8 to 10 minutes or until browned and tender, shaking occasionally during cooking. Return to large bowl.

4 Add mushrooms to basket. Cook 6 to 8 minutes or until browned, shaking occasionally during cooking.

5 Combine sour cream, lime juice, chili powder and remaining ½ teaspoon salt in small bowl; mix well.

6 For each taco, spread 1 tablespoon beans and 1 teaspoon sour cream mixture over tortilla; top with about 3 mushroom slices and ¼ cup cauliflower. Top with cilantro and pickled onions, if desired. Fold in half.

Makes 8 tacos

PICKLED RED ONIONS

Thinly slice 1 small red onion; place in large glass jar. Add ¼ cup white wine vinegar or white vinegar, 2 tablespoons water, 1 teaspoon sugar and 1 teaspoon salt. Seal jar; shake well. Refrigerate at least 1 hour or up to 1 week. Makes about ½ cup.

Coconut Shrimp

DIPPING SAUCE

- ½ cup orange marmalade
- ⅓ cup Thai chili sauce
- 1 teaspoon prepared horseradish
- ½ teaspoon salt

SHRIMP

- 1 cup flat beer
- 1 cup all-purpose flour
- 2 cups sweetened flaked coconut, divided
- 2 tablespoons sugar
- 16 to 20 large raw shrimp, peeled, deveined and patted dry

1 For sauce, combine marmalade, chili sauce, horseradish and salt in small bowl; mix well.

2 For shrimp, whisk beer, flour, ½ cup coconut and sugar in large bowl until well blended. Place remaining 1½ cups coconut in medium bowl.

3 Preheat air fryer to 390°F. Line basket with parchment paper; spray with nonstick cooking spray.

4 Dip shrimp in beer batter, then in coconut, turning to coat completely.

5 Cook shrimp in batches 6 to 8 minutes or until golden brown, turning halfway through cooking. Serve with dipping sauce.

Makes 4 servings

Spicy Lemon Almond Chicken

½ teaspoon paprika

½ teaspoon black pepper

¼ teaspoon salt

4 boneless skinless chicken breasts (about 4 ounces each), pounded to ¼-inch thickness

¼ cup water

2 tablespoons lemon juice

2 tablespoons butter

2 teaspoons Worcestershire sauce

½ teaspoon grated lemon peel

1 ounce slivered almonds, toasted*

To toast almonds in air fryer, cook in small dish or ramekin at 325°F 4 minutes or until lightly browned and fragrant, shaking frequently. To toast almonds in skillet, cook over medium heat about 5 minutes or until lightly browned and fragrant, stirring frequently.

1 Combine paprika, pepper and salt in small bowl; mix well. Pound chicken to ¼-inch thickness between two sheets of plastic wrap with meat mallet or rolling pin. Sprinkle paprika mixture over both sides of chicken.

2 Preheat air fryer to 370°F. Spray basket with nonstick cooking spray.

3 Cook chicken 12 to 15 minutes or until lightly browned and no longer pink in center. Remove to plate; tent with foil to keep warm.

4 Combine water, lemon juice, butter and Worcestershire sauce in small skillet; cook and stir over medium-high heat until sauce is reduced to ¼ cup. Remove from heat, stir in lemon peel. Spoon sauce over chicken; sprinkle with almonds.

Makes 4 servings

Chicken Air-Fried Steak with Creamy Gravy

STEAK

½ cup all-purpose flour
½ teaspoon coarse salt
½ teaspoon onion powder
¼ teaspoon paprika
¼ teaspoon ground red pepper
⅛ teaspoon black pepper
1 large egg
¼ cup water
1 pound cube steak, cut into 4 pieces

GRAVY

1½ tablespoons butter
2 to 3 tablespoons all-purpose flour
¾ cup chicken broth
½ cup milk
Salt and black pepper

1 For steak, combine ½ cup flour, ½ teaspoon salt, onion powder, paprika, ground red pepper and ⅛ teaspoon black pepper in shallow dish. Beat egg and water in another shallow dish.

2 Coat steaks with flour mixture, then in egg mixture, letting excess drip back into dish. Dip again in flour mixture to coat. Spray generously with nonstick cooking spray.

3 Preheat air fryer to 370°F. Spray basket with cooking spray or line with parchment paper and spray with cooking spray.

4 Cook steak in batches 12 to 14 minutes or until browned and no longer pink in center, turning halfway through cooking. Remove to plate; tent with foil to keep warm.

5 Meanwhile, for gravy, melt butter in small skillet over medium heat. Add 2 tablespoons flour, broth and milk; cook and stir until slightly thickened. If necessary, add additional 1 tablespoon flour to thicken. Season with salt and black pepper. Serve steaks with gravy.

Makes 4 servings

Teriyaki Salmon →

¼ cup dark sesame oil
¼ cup soy sauce
Juice of 1 lemon
2 tablespoons packed brown sugar
1 clove garlic, minced
2 salmon fillets (4 to 6 ounces each)
Toasted sesame seeds and green onions (optional)

1 Whisk oil, soy sauce, lemon juice, brown sugar and garlic in medium bowl until well blended.

2 Place salmon in large resealable food storage bag. Pour marinade over salmon; seal bag and turn to coat. Refrigerate at least 2 hours.

3 Preheat air fryer to 390°F. Spray basket with nonstick cooking spray.

4 Cook salmon 8 to 10 minutes or until top is crisp and fish begins to flake when tested with fork. Sprinkle with sesame seeds and green onions, if desired.

Makes 2 servings

Blue Cheese Stuffed Chicken Breasts

½ cup crumbled blue cheese
2 tablespoons butter, softened, divided
¾ teaspoon dried thyme
Salt and black pepper
4 bone-in skin-on chicken breasts
1 tablespoon lemon juice

1 Combine blue cheese, 1 tablespoon butter and thyme in small bowl; mix well. Season with salt and pepper.

2 Loosen chicken skin by pushing fingers between skin and meat, taking care not to tear skin. Spread cheese mixture under skin; massage skin to spread mixture evenly over chicken breast.

3 Melt remaining 1 tablespoon butter in small bowl; stir in lemon juice until blended. Brush mixture over chicken. Sprinkle with salt and pepper.

4 Preheat air fryer to 370°F. Cook chicken 15 to 20 minutes or until cooked through (165°F).

Makes 4 servings

Greek Chicken Burgers with Cucumber Yogurt Sauce

SAUCE

- ½ cup plus 2 tablespoons plain Greek yogurt
- ½ medium cucumber, peeled, seeded and finely chopped
- Juice of ½ lemon
- 3 cloves garlic, minced, divided
- 2 teaspoons finely chopped fresh mint *or* ½ teaspoon dried mint
- ¼ teaspoon salt
- ⅛ teaspoon ground white pepper

BURGERS

- 1 pound ground chicken
- ¾ cup crumbled feta cheese
- 4 large Kalamata olives, minced
- 1 egg
- ¾ teaspoon dried oregano
- ¼ teaspoon black pepper
- Mixed greens (optional)
- Fresh mint leaves (optional)

1 For sauce, combine yogurt, cucumber, lemon juice, 2 cloves garlic, 2 teaspoons chopped mint, salt and white pepper in medium bowl; mix well. Cover and refrigerate until ready to serve.

2 For burgers, combine chicken, cheese, olives, egg, oregano, black pepper and remaining 1 clove garlic in large bowl; mix well. Shape mixture into four patties.

3 Preheat air fryer to 370°F. Spray basket with nonstick cooking spray.

4 Cook patties 12 to 15 minutes or until cooked through (165°F). Serve burgers with sauce and mixed greens, if desired; garnish with fresh mint.

Makes 4 servings

Milanese Pork Chops

2 tablespoons all-purpose flour

½ teaspoon salt

½ teaspoon black pepper

1 egg

1 teaspoon water

¼ cup seasoned dry bread crumbs

¼ cup grated Parmesan cheese

4 boneless pork loin chops, cut ¾ inch thick

Lemon wedges

1 Combine flour, salt and pepper in shallow dish. Beat egg and water in another shallow dish. Combine bread crumbs and cheese in third shallow dish.

2 Coat both sides of pork chops first in flour mixture, then in egg mixture, letting excess drip back into dish. Coat with bread crumb mixture, pressing to adhere. Place on plate; refrigerate 15 minutes.

3 Preheat air fryer to 400°F. Place pork chops in single layer in basket; spray lightly with nonstick cooking spray.

4 Cook pork chops in single layer 7 minutes; turn and cook 5 minutes or until pork is 145°F and barely pink in center. Let stand 5 minutes before serving. Serve with lemon wedges.

Makes 4 servings

Zesty Italian Chicken Nuggets →

4 **boneless skinless chicken breasts (4 to 6 ounces each)**
½ **cup zesty Italian salad dressing**
2 **tablespoons honey**
1 **teaspoon salt**
½ **teaspoon black pepper**

1 Cut chicken into 1-inch pieces. Place in large resealable food storage bag.

2 Whisk dressing, honey, salt and pepper in medium bowl until well blended. Pour over chicken; seal bag and turn to coat. Marinate in refrigerator 30 minutes to 1 hour.

3 Preheat air fryer to 370°F. Line basket with parchment paper. Remove chicken from marinade; discard marinade.

4 Cook chicken in batches 10 to 12 minutes or until cooked through, shaking halfway through cooking.

Makes 4 servings

Big Kid Shrimp

½ **cup plain dry bread crumbs**
¼ **cup grated Parmesan cheese**
½ **teaspoon paprika**
½ **teaspoon salt**
⅛ **teaspoon black pepper**
2 **tablespoons butter, melted**
1 **pound large raw shrimp, peeled and deveined**
½ **cup mayonnaise**
½ **cup ketchup**
1 **tablespoon sweet pickle relish**

1 Combine bread crumbs, cheese, paprika, salt and pepper in large bowl. Stir in butter until well blended. Add shrimp; toss to coat, pressing crumb mixture to adhere.

2 Preheat air fryer to 390°F. Line basket with parchment paper; spray with nonstick cooking spray.

3 Cook shrimp in batches 6 to 8 minutes or until golden brown, turning halfway through cooking.

4 Combine mayonnaise, ketchup and relish in small bowl; mix well. Serve with shrimp.

Makes 4 servings

Easy Asian Pork Tenderloin →

3 tablespoons barbecue
   sauce
1 tablespoon soy sauce
1 tablespoon dry sherry
2 cloves garlic, minced
¼ teaspoon red pepper
   flakes
2 pork tenderloins
   (about 1 pound each)

1 Whisk barbecue sauce, soy sauce, sherry, garlic and red pepper flakes in small bowl until well blended.

2 Preheat air fryer to 350°F. Spray basket with nonstick cooking spray.

3 Cut pork tenderloins in half crosswise. Brush half of barbecue sauce mixture over pork.

4 Cook pork in single layer 9 minutes; turn and brush with remaining sauce mixture. Cook about 9 minutes or until pork is 145°F. Remove to cutting board; tent with foil and let stand 10 minutes before slicing.

Makes 6 to 8 servings

Crispy Mustard Chicken

4 bone-in chicken breasts
½ teaspoon salt
¼ teaspoon black pepper
¼ cup Dijon mustard
½ cup panko bread crumbs
   or plain dry bread
   crumbs

1 Preheat air fryer to 370°F. Line basket with foil; spray with nonstick cooking spray.

2 Season chicken with salt and pepper. Cook 20 minutes.

3 Brush chicken generously with mustard. Sprinkle with panko, pressing panko into mustard. Cook 6 to 8 minutes or until chicken is golden brown and cooked through (165°F).

Makes 4 servings

Air-Fried Salmon Bites with Broccoli

2 eggs

1 cup plain dry
   bread crumbs

¾ teaspoon salt, divided

1 pound skinless salmon
   fillet, cut into 1-inch
   pieces

2 cups broccoli florets

1 tablespoon olive oil

   Sweet and sour sauce or
   favorite dipping sauce
   (optional)

1 Beat eggs in shallow dish. Combine bread crumbs and ½ teaspoon salt in another shallow dish. Dip salmon in eggs, letting excess drip back into dish. Roll in bread crumbs to coat. Spray fish lightly with nonstick cooking spray.

2 Preheat air fryer to 390°F. Spray basket with cooking spray.

3 Cook fish in batches 3 to 4 minutes. Turn and spray with cooking spray; cook 3 to 4 minutes or until golden brown. Remove to plate; tent with foil to keep warm.

4 Drizzle broccoli with oil in large bowl; toss to coat. Sprinkle with remaining ¼ teaspoon salt.

5 Cook broccoli 6 to 8 minutes or until browned and crisp, shaking halfway through cooking. Serve broccoli with salmon and sweet and sour sauce, if desired.

Makes 4 servings

VARIATION

For additional flavor, substitute garlic-herb or Italian-seasoned bread crumbs for the plain.

Lemon-Pepper Chicken →

⅓ cup lemon juice

¼ cup finely chopped onion

2 tablespoons olive oil

1 tablespoon packed brown sugar

1 tablespoon black pepper

3 cloves garlic, minced

2 teaspoons grated lemon peel

½ teaspoon salt

4 boneless skinless chicken breasts (4 to 6 ounces each)

1 Combine lemon juice, onion, oil, brown sugar, pepper, garlic, lemon peel and salt in small bowl; mix well.

2 Place chicken in large resealable food storage bag. Pour marinade over chicken; seal bag and turn to coat. Refrigerate at least 4 hours or overnight.

3 Preheat air fryer to 370°F. Line basket with parchment paper or foil; spray with nonstick cooking spray. Remove chicken from marinade; discard marinade.

4 Cook chicken in single layer 15 to 20 minutes or until browned and no longer pink in center.

Makes 4 servings

Roasted Almond Tilapia

2 tilapia or Boston scrod fillets (4 to 6 ounces each)

⅛ teaspoon salt

2 teaspoons mustard

¼ cup all-purpose flour

2 tablespoons chopped almonds

Paprika

Lemon wedges (optional)

1 Season tilapia with salt. Spread mustard over fish.

2 Combine flour and almonds in small bowl; mix well. Sprinkle over fish, pressing gently to adhere. Sprinkle with paprika.

3 Preheat air fryer to 370°F. Line basket with parchment paper.

4 Cook fish 12 to 15 minutes or until fish is opaque in center and begins to flake when tested with fork. Serve with lemon wedges, if desired.

Makes 2 servings

Pork with Spicy Orange Cranberry Sauce

1 teaspoon chili powder

½ teaspoon salt

½ teaspoon ground cumin

¼ teaspoon ground allspice

¼ teaspoon black pepper

4 boneless pork chops
   (about 4 ounces each,
   1 inch thick)

1 tablespoon canola oil

1 cup whole berry
   cranberry sauce

½ teaspoon grated
   orange peel

¼ teaspoon ground
   cinnamon

⅛ teaspoon red pepper
   flakes

1 Combine chili powder, salt, cumin, allspice and black pepper in small bowl; mix well. Pat pork chops dry with paper towel. Drizzle with oil; sprinkle both sides of pork chops with spice mixture, coating evenly.

2 Preheat air fryer to 380°F. Spray basket with nonstick cooking spray.

3 Cook pork chops in single layer 6 minutes; turn and cook 4 minutes or until pork is 145°F and barely pink in center.

4 Meanwhile, combine cranberry sauce, orange peel, cinnamon and red pepper flakes in small bowl; mix well. Serve sauce with pork chops.

Makes 4 servings

Black Bean and Rice Stuffed Poblano Peppers

4 poblano peppers

1 can (about 15 ounces) black beans, rinsed and drained

1 cup cooked brown rice

¾ cup shredded Cheddar cheese or pepper-Jack cheese, divided

⅔ cup chunky salsa

¼ teaspoon salt

1 Cut thin slice from one side of each pepper; remove seeds and membranes. Chop pepper slices; set aside.

2 Preheat air fryer to 380°F. Spray peppers with nonstick cooking spray. Cook 6 to 8 minutes or until skins are slightly softened. Remove to plate. *Reduce temperature of air fryer to 350°F.*

3 Combine beans, rice, ½ cup cheese, salsa, chopped poblano pepper and salt in medium bowl; mix well. Spoon mixture into peppers, mounding in center.

4 Line basket with parchment paper; place filled peppers in basket. (Make sure there is space between peppers for air circulation, or cook in two batches.)

5 Cook peppers 6 to 8 minutes or until filling is heated through. Sprinkle with remaining ¼ cup cheese; cook 2 minutes or until cheese is melted.

Makes 4 servings

Garlicky Air-Fried Chicken Thighs

1 egg
2 tablespoons water
1 cup plain dry bread
   crumbs
1 teaspoon salt
1 teaspoon garlic powder
½ teaspoon black pepper
¼ teaspoon ground
   red pepper
8 bone-in chicken thighs
   (about 3 pounds),
   skin removed

1 Beat egg and water in shallow dish. Combine bread crumbs, salt, garlic powder, black pepper and red pepper in another shallow dish.

2 Dip chicken in egg mixture, letting excess drip back into dish. Roll in bread crumb mixture to coat.

3 Preheat air fryer to 390°F. Spray chicken lightly with nonstick cooking spray.

4 Cook chicken 20 to 22 minutes or until golden brown and cooked through (165°F).

Makes 4 servings

VARIATIONS

Substitute seasoned bread crumbs for the plain bread crumbs, garlic powder, ground red pepper, salt and black pepper. Or, substitute your favorite dried herbs or spices for the garlic powder and ground red pepper.

SIDE DISHES

Parmesan Potato Wedges

2 pounds unpeeled red
  potatoes
2 tablespoons butter, melted
1½ teaspoons dried oregano
½ teaspoon salt
¼ teaspoon black pepper
¼ cup grated Parmesan
  cheese

1 Boil potatoes in large saucepan of salted water 8 to 10 minutes or until fork-tender; drain and cool completely.

2 Cut cooled potatoes into wedges; place in large bowl. Add butter, oregano, salt and pepper; toss gently to coat.

3 Preheat air fryer to 390°F. Line basket with parchment paper.

4 Cook potatoes 10 to 12 minutes or until golden brown, shaking occasionally during cooking.

5 Return potatoes to large bowl; sprinkle with cheese and toss to coat.

Makes 4 to 6 servings

Air-Fryer Mexican Corn Ribs

2 ears corn

¼ cup (½ stick) butter, softened

½ teaspoon chili powder

¼ teaspoon garlic powder

¼ teaspoon black pepper

¼ cup mayonnaise

2 teaspoons lime juice

1 teaspoon hot pepper sauce

2 tablespoons crumbled cotija or feta cheese

1 tablespoon chopped fresh cilantro

1 Husk corn and remove silk. Rinse and dry corn. Use large knife to cut ears of corn in half horizontally, then cut each half lengthwise into quarters to create four "ribs."

2 Combine butter, chili powder, garlic powder and black pepper in small bowl; mix well. Brush mixture over corn.

3 Preheat air fryer to 390°F. Line basket with parchment paper.

4 Cook corn 12 to 14 minutes or until charred, turning halfway through cooking. Remove to plate.

5 Meanwhile, combine mayonnaise, lime juice and hot pepper sauce in small bowl; mix well. Brush over hot corn; sprinkle with cheese and cilantro.

Makes 4 servings

Potato Balls

2 cups refrigerated leftover mashed potatoes*

2 tablespoons all-purpose flour, plus additional for rolling

⅔ cup shredded Cheddar cheese

¼ cup chopped green onions

2 eggs

½ teaspoon salt

¼ teaspoon black pepper

1½ cups seasoned dry bread crumbs

Chopped fresh chives (optional)

*If you don't have leftover potatoes, prepare 2 cups instant mashed potatoes and refrigerate at least 1 hour.

1 Combine potatoes, 2 tablespoons flour, cheese and green onions in large bowl; mix well. Scoop out about 2 tablespoons mixture and roll into a 1-inch ball, adding additional flour if necessary to prevent sticking. Repeat with remaining potato mixture to create about 20 balls.

2 Beat eggs, salt and pepper in shallow dish. Place bread crumbs in another shallow dish. Dip potato balls in egg, letting excess drip back into dish. Roll in bread crumbs to coat. Place on baking sheet; refrigerate 30 minutes.

3 Preheat air fryer to 390°F. Spray basket with nonstick cooking spray.

4 Cook potato balls in batches 8 to 10 minutes or until well browned, shaking halfway through cooking. Garnish with chives.

Makes about 20 balls

Crispy Brussels Sprouts →

1 pound Brussels sprouts, trimmed and halved

¼ cup ground almonds

2 tablespoons grated Parmesan cheese

1½ tablespoons olive oil

1 tablespoon everything bagel seasoning or favorite seasoning blend

1 Preheat air fryer to 370°F.

2 Combine Brussels sprouts, almonds, cheese, oil and bagel seasoning in medium bowl; toss to coat.

3 Cook Brussels sprouts 8 to 10 minutes or until lighlty browned and crisp, shaking occasionally during cooking.

Makes 4 servings

Sweet Potato Fries

2 sweet potatoes, peeled and cut into strips

1 tablespoon olive oil

¼ teaspoon coarse salt

¼ teaspoon black pepper

1 Preheat air fryer to 390°F. Spray basket with nonstick cooking spray.

2 Combine sweet potatoes, oil, salt and pepper in medium bowl; toss to coat.

3 Cook sweet potatoes 10 to 12 minutes or until lightly browned, shaking occasionally during cooking.

Makes 2 servings

Cauliflower "Hash Brown" Patties →

4 slices bacon

1 package (about 12 ounces) cauliflower rice

½ cup finely chopped onion

½ cup finely chopped red and/or green bell pepper

½ cup (2 ounces) shredded Cheddar cheese

⅓ cup all-purpose flour

1 egg

1 tablespoon chopped fresh chives

1 teaspoon salt

½ teaspoon black pepper

1 Preheat air fryer to 400°F. Cook bacon 8 to 10 minutes; remove paper towel-lined plate. Crumble into small pieces.

2 Place cauliflower in large bowl. Add bacon, onion, bell pepper, cheese, flour, egg, chives, salt and black pepper; mix well. Shape mixture into eight patties; place on baking sheet. Freeze 30 minutes.

3 Preheat air fryer to 370°F. Spray basket with nonstick cooking spray.

4 Cook patties in batches 12 to 15 minutes or until browned, turning halfway through cooking.

Makes 8 servings

Roasted Butternut Squash

1 pound butternut squash, peeled and cut into 1-inch pieces (about 4 cups)

2 medium onions, coarsely chopped

8 ounces carrots, peeled and cut into ½-inch diagonal slices (about 2 cups)

1 tablespoon olive oil

1 tablespoon packed dark brown sugar

¾ teaspoon salt

¼ teaspoon black pepper

1 Preheat air fryer to 390°F. Spray basket with nonstick cooking spray.

2 Combine squash, onions and carrots, oil, brown sugar, salt and pepper in large bowl; toss to coat.

3 Cook vegetables 20 to 25 minutes or until tender and browned, shaking occasionally during cooking.

Makes 4 servings

Italian-Style Roasted Vegetables

1 small eggplant, cut into chunks

1 small zucchini, cut into chunks

1 small red bell pepper, cut into chunks

1 small yellow bell pepper, cut into chunks

1 small onion, cut into chunks

10 cloves garlic, peeled

2 tablespoons olive oil

1 teaspoon white vinegar

½ teaspoon salt

½ teaspoon dried basil

½ teaspoon dried oregano

¼ teaspoon red pepper flakes

Shredded Parmesan cheese (optional)

1 Preheat air fryer to 390°F. Spray basket with nonstick cooking spray.

2 Combine eggplant, zucchini, bell peppers, onion and garlic in large bowl. Add oil and vinegar, salt, basil, oregano and red pepper flakes; toss to coat.

3 Cook vegetables in batches 12 to 15 minutes or until tender and browned, shaking halfway through cooking. Sprinkle with cheese, if desired.

Makes 6 servings

Orange and Maple-Glazed Beets

4 **medium beets**

¼ **cup orange juice**

3 **tablespoons balsamic
   or cider vinegar**

2 **tablespoons maple syrup**

2 **teaspoons grated orange
   peel, divided**

1 **teaspoon Dijon mustard**

Salt and black pepper

1 **to 2 tablespoons chopped
   fresh mint (optional)**

1 Peel beets; cut in half lengthwise and then cut into wedges. Place in large bowl.

2 Whisk orange juice, vinegar, maple syrup, 1 teaspoon orange peel and mustard in small bowl until well blended. Pour half of mixture over beets; toss to coat.

3 Preheat air fryer to 390°F.

4 Cook beets 22 to 25 minutes or until tender, shaking occasionally during cooking.

5 Remove to serving dish; pour remaining orange juice mixture over beets. Season with salt and pepper; toss to coat. Sprinkle with remaining 1 teaspoon orange peel and mint, if desired.

Makes 4 servings

Crispy Fries with Herbed Dipping Sauce

2 large baking potatoes,
   cut into ¼-inch strips
1 tablespoon vegetable oil
½ teaspoon coarse salt
  Herbed Dipping Sauce
  (recipe follows)

1 Combine potatoes, oil and salt in large bowl; toss to coat.

2 Preheat air fryer to 390°F.

3 Cook potatoes in batches 12 to 15 minutes or until golden brown and crisp, shaking occasionally during cooking.

4 Meanwhile, prepare Herbed Dipping Sauce. Serve potatoes immediately with sauce.

Makes 3 servings

HERBED DIPPING SAUCE

Combine ¼ cup mayonnaise, 1 tablespoon chopped fresh herbs (such as basil, parsley, oregano and/or dill), ¼ teaspoon salt and ⅛ teaspoon black pepper in small bowl; mix well.

Hush Puppies →

1½ cups yellow cornmeal
½ cup all-purpose flour
2 teaspoons baking powder
¾ teaspoon salt
1 cup milk
1 small onion, minced
1 egg, lightly beaten
Ketchup and/or ranch
   dressing (optional)

1 Combine cornmeal, flour, baking powder and salt in medium bowl; mix well. Add milk, onion and egg; stir until well blended. Let batter stand 5 to 10 minutes.

2 Preheat air fryer to 390°F. Line basket with parchment paper.

3 Roll or drop batter by tablespoonfuls onto parchment-lined basket.

4 Cook hush puppies in batches 8 to 10 minutes or until golden brown. Serve warm with ketchup, if desired.

Makes about 24 hush puppies

Bacon-Roasted Brussels Sprouts

1 pound Brussels sprouts,
   trimmed and halved
2 slices bacon, cut into
   ½-inch pieces
2 teaspoons packed
   brown sugar
   Salt and black pepper

1 Preheat air fryer to 390°F.

2 Combine Brussels sprouts, bacon and brown sugar in large bowl; mix well.

3 Cook Brussels sprouts 15 to 18 minutes or until golden brown, shaking occasionally during cooking. Season with salt and pepper.

Makes 4 servings

Eggplant Steaks

1 small to medium eggplant, cut crosswise into ¾-inch slices

2 tablespoons olive oil

1 tablespoon herb seasoning blend or garlic herb seasoning

¼ cup (½ stick) butter, melted

2 tablespoons grated Parmesan cheese, plus additional for garnish

1 tablespoon minced garlic

½ teaspoon salt

¼ teaspoon black pepper

1 tablespoon fresh chopped parsley

Marinara sauce, warmed (optional)

1 Preheat air fryer to 390°F. Spray basket with nonstick cooking spray.

2 Place eggplant on large plate. Brush both sides with oil; sprinkle with seasoning blend.

3 Cook eggplant in single layer 14 to 16 minutes or until golden brown and crisp around edges, turning halfway through cooking.

4 Combine butter, cheese, garlic, salt and pepper in small bowl; mix well. Brush over warm eggplant; sprinkle with parsley and additional cheese. Serve with marinara sauce, if desired.

Makes 4 to 6 servings

Cinnamon-Honey Glazed Carrot Chips →

¼ cup honey
2 tablespoons butter
1 teaspoon ground
    cinnamon
½ teaspoon ground nutmeg
¼ teaspoon salt
1 package (16 ounces)
    carrot chips or
    baby carrots

1 Combine honey and butter in medium microwavable bowl; microwave on HIGH 30 seconds until melted. Add cinnamon, nutmeg and salt; stir until blended.

2 Add carrots to honey mixture; toss to coat.

3 Preheat air fryer to 390°F. Line basket with parchment paper.

4 Cook carrots in single layer 12 to 15 minutes or until slightly tender and browned, shaking halfway through cooking.

Makes 6 servings

Butternut Squash Fries

½ teaspoon salt
½ teaspoon garlic powder
¼ teaspoon ground
    red pepper
1 butternut squash
    (about 2½ pounds),
    peeled, seeded and
    cut into thin strips
2 teaspoons vegetable oil

1 Preheat air fryer to 390°F. Combine salt, garlic powder and red pepper in small bowl; mix well.

2 Place squash in large bowl. Drizzle with oil and sprinkle with seasoning mix; toss to coat.

3 Cook squash in batches 16 to 18 minutes or until tender and beginning to brown, shaking halfway through cooking.

Makes 4 servings

Garlic Air-Fried Fries →

2 large potatoes, peeled and cut into matchstick strips
2 teaspoons plus 1 tablespoon olive oil, divided
1½ teaspoons minced garlic
½ teaspoon dried parsley flakes
½ teaspoon salt
¼ teaspoon black pepper
Ketchup and/or blue cheese dressing (optional)

1 Preheat air fryer to 390°F. Line basket with parchment paper.

2 Combine potatoes and 2 teaspoons oil in medium bowl; toss to coat.

3 Cook potatoes in batches 8 to 10 minutes or until golden brown and crisp, shaking occasionally during cooking.

4 Meanwhile, combine remaining 1 tablespoon oil, garlic, parsley flakes, salt and pepper in medium bowl; mix well.

5 Add warm fries to garlic mixture; toss to coat. Serve immediately with ketchup and blue cheese dressing, if desired.

Makes 4 servings

Roasted Asparagus

1 bunch asparagus spears (14 to 16 ounces), trimmed
1 tablespoon olive oil
½ teaspoon salt
¼ teaspoon black pepper
¼ cup shredded Asiago or Parmesan cheese (optional)

1 Place asparagus in shallow dish or rimmed plate. Drizzle with oil, rolling spears to coat. Sprinkle with salt and pepper.

2 Preheat air fryer to 390°F.

3 Cook asparagus in batches 8 to 10 minutes or until tender, shaking occasionally during cooking. Sprinkle with cheese, if desired.

Makes 4 servings

Roasted Green Beans and Mushrooms →

1 pound fresh green beans, trimmed

1 large onion, cut into ¼-inch slices

8 ounces sliced mushrooms

1 teaspoon minced garlic

½ teaspoon salt

¼ teaspoon black pepper

1 tablespoon olive oil

1 Preheat air fryer to 370°F. Spray basket with nonstick cooking spray.

2 Combine green beans, onion, mushrooms, garlic, salt and pepper in large bowl. Drizzle with oil; toss to coat.

3 Cook vegetables 14 to 16 minutes or until tender and browned, shaking halfway through cooking.

Makes 4 to 6 servings

Air-Fried Corn on the Cob

2 teaspoons butter, melted

½ teaspoon chopped fresh parsley

¼ teaspoon salt

¼ teaspoon black pepper

2 ears corn, husks and silks removed

Grated Parmesan cheese (optional)

1 Preheat air fryer to 390°F. Combine butter, parsley, salt and pepper in small bowl; mix well.

2 Brush corn with butter mixture. Wrap each ear of corn in foil.*

3 Cook corn 6 to 8 minutes, turning halfway through cooking. Sprinkle with cheese, if desired.

*If your air fryer basket is too small to fit whole ears of corn, break them in half to fit.

Makes 2 servings

Curried Cauliflower and Brussels Sprouts →

2 pounds cauliflower florets

12 ounces Brussels sprouts, trimmed and halved

⅓ cup olive oil

2½ tablespoons curry powder

½ teaspoon sea salt

½ teaspoon black pepper

½ cup chopped fresh cilantro

1 Combine cauliflower, Brussels sprouts and oil in large bowl; toss to coat. Sprinkle with curry powder, salt and pepper; toss to coat.

2 Preheat air fryer to 370°F. Line basket with foil.

3 Cook vegetables in batches 12 to 15 minutes or until golden brown, shaking halfway through cooking.

4 Add cilantro; stir until blended.

Makes 8 servings

Herbed Potatoes and Onions

2 pounds red potatoes, cut into 1½-inch pieces

1 sweet onion, such as Vidalia or Walla Walla, coarsely chopped

2 cloves garlic, minced

½ teaspoon salt

¼ teaspoon black pepper

2 tablespoons olive oil

¼ cup packed chopped mixed fresh herbs, such as basil, chives, parsley, oregano, rosemary leaves, sage, tarragon and thyme

1 Combine potatoes, onion, garlic, salt and pepper in large bowl. Drizzle with oil; toss to coat.

2 Preheat air fryer to 390°F. Line basket with foil.

3 Cook vegetables 18 to 20 minutes or until potatoes are tender and browned, shaking occasionally during cooking.

4 Return vegetables to large bowl. Add fresh herbs; toss to coat.

Makes 4 to 6 servings

SWEET TREATS

Fried Pineapple with Toasted Coconut

1 large pineapple, cored and cut into 1-inch pieces

½ cup packed brown sugar

1 teaspoon ground cinnamon

½ teaspoon ground nutmeg

½ cup toasted coconut*

Vanilla ice cream

Maraschino cherries (optional)

*To toast coconut in air fryer, place coconut in ramekin. Cook in preheated 350°F air fryer 2 to 3 minutes or until lightly browned.

1 Place pineapple in large bowl. Combine brown sugar, cinnamon and nutmeg in small bowl; mix well. Sprinkle over pineapple; toss to coat. Refrigerate 30 minutes.

2 Preheat air fryer to 370°F. Spray basket with nonstick cooking spray.

3 Cook pineapple 6 to 8 minutes or browned and slightly crisp, shaking halfway through cooking.

4 Sprinkle pineapple with coconut; serve with ice cream. Top with cherries, if desired.

Makes 8 servings

Bloomin' Baked Apples

2 apples
2 tablespoons butter, melted
1 tablespoon granulated sugar
1 tablespoon packed brown sugar
½ teaspoon ground cinnamon
Vanilla ice cream (optional)
Caramel sauce, warmed (optional)

1 Slice about ½ inch off tops of apples. Use paring knife or apple cutter to cut about eight vertical slices in each apple, being careful not to cut all the way through to bottom. Remove and discard apple cores and seeds.

2 Preheat air fryer to 370°F.

3 Combine butter, granulated sugar, brown sugar and cinnamon in small bowl; mix well. Place apples in small baking dish that fits inside air fryer. Brush apples with butter mixture, letting mixture drip down between slices.

4 Cook apples 15 to 20 minutes or until softened and lightly browned. Serve warm with ice cream; drizzle with caramel sauce, if desired.

Makes 2 servings

Shortbread Cookie Sticks

1¼ cups all-purpose flour

3 tablespoons sugar

¼ teaspoon salt

½ cup (1 stick) butter

½ cup chocolate chips

1 tablespoon whipping cream

¼ cup colored sprinkles (optional)

1 Combine flour, sugar and salt in large bowl; mix well. Cut in butter with pastry cutter or two knives until fine crumbs form. Use damp hands to shape dough into a ball; knead until smooth.

2 Roll out dough to ½-inch thickness on lightly floured work surface. Cut into 4×½-inch sticks.

3 Preheat air fryer to 350°F.

4 Cook cookie sticks in batches 5 to 7 minutes or until lightly browned. Remove to wire rack to cool completely.

5 Combine chocolate chips and cream in small microwavable bowl; microwave on HIGH 30 seconds or until chocolate is melted. Stir until mixture is blended and smooth. Dip sticks in chocolate; top with sprinkles, if desired. Place on parchment-lined cookie sheet or plate; refrigerate until chocolate is set.

Makes 18 cookies

Apple Pie Egg Rolls

3 Granny Smith apples
   or other tart apples,
   peeled and chopped
½ cup packed brown sugar
1¾ teaspoons ground
   cinnamon, divided
1 teaspoon cornstarch
¼ teaspoon salt
½ teaspoon vanilla
8 egg roll wrappers
2 tablespoons water
1 teaspoon granulated sugar
1 tablespoon butter, melted
   Caramel sauce, warmed
   (optional)

1 Combine apples, brown sugar, 1½ teaspoons cinnamon, cornstarch and salt in medium saucepan; cook over high heat 3 minutes, stirring occasionally. Reduce heat to low; cook 5 to 6 minutes or until apples are tender. Remove from heat; stir in vanilla.

2 Place one egg roll wrapper on work surface with one corner facing you. Moisten edges of wrapper with fingertips dipped in water. Spoon about 1 tablespoon apple mixture in center of wrapper. Fold bottom point of wrapper up over filling, then fold in sides and roll up to enclose filling. Repeat with remaining wrappers and filling.

3 Combine granulated sugar and remaining ¼ teaspoon cinnamon in small bowl; mix well. Brush egg rolls lightly with butter; sprinkle with cinnamon-sugar.

4 Preheat air fryer to 370°F. Spray basket with nonstick cooking spray.

5 Cook egg rolls in single layer, seam sides down, 8 to 10 minutes or until lightly browned. Cool slightly; serve warm with caramel sauce, if desired.

Makes 8 egg rolls

Gooey Double Chocolate Brownies

½ cup (1 stick) butter, melted

¾ cup unsweetened cocoa powder

1 cup sugar

2 eggs

⅔ cup all-purpose flour

½ teaspoon salt

½ cup semisweet chocolate chunks or chips

Vanilla ice cream (optional)

1 Spray 7-inch round cake pan* with nonstick cooking spray. Line bottom of pan with parchment paper; spray with cooking spray.

2 Place butter in medium microwavable bowl; microwave until melted. Stir in cocoa until well blended.

3 Beat sugar and eggs in large bowl until well blended. Add cocoa mixture; stir until smooth. Add flour and salt; stir until blended. Stir in chocolate chunks. Spread batter in prepared pan; smooth top. Cover with foil. Preheat air fryer to 310°F.

4 Cook 45 minutes. Uncover; cook 10 minutes or until toothpick inserted into center comes out with fudgy crumbs. Cool on wire rack 15 minutes. Serve warm or at room temperature with ice cream, if desired.

*A 6-inch cake pan may be used; baking time will be slightly longer.

Makes 8 servings

Bacon S'more Bundles →

1¼ cups mini marshmallows

¾ cup semisweet chocolate chips

¾ cup coarsely crushed graham crackers (5 whole graham crackers)

4 slices bacon, crisp-cooked and crumbled

1 package (about 17 ounces) frozen puff pastry (2 sheets), thawed

1 Combine marshmallows, chocolate chips, graham crackers and bacon in medium bowl; mix well.

2 Unfold pastry on lightly floured surface. Roll out each pastry sheet into 12-inch square; cut each sheet into four 6-inch squares. Place scant ½ cup marshmallow mixture in center of each square.

3 Brush edges of pastry squares lightly with water. Bring edges together up over filling; twist tightly to seal.

4 Preheat air fryer to 370°F. Cook pastries in batches 6 to 8 minutes or until golden brown. Remove to wire rack to cool 5 minutes. Serve warm.

Makes 8 servings

Toasted Pound Cake with Berries and Cream

1 package (about 10 ounces) frozen pound cake

2 tablespoons butter, melted

1 cup fresh blackberries or blueberries

1 cup fresh raspberries or strawberries

Whipped cream

1 Preheat air fryer to 370°F.

2 Cut pound cake into eight slices. Brush both sides of cake slices with butter.

3 Cook cake in batches 5 to 7 minutes or until lightly browned, turning halfway through cooking.

4 Serve cake warm with berries and whipped cream.

Makes 4 servings

Apple Fries with Caramel Sauce

APPLE FRIES

- ½ cup all-purpose flour
- 2 eggs
- 1 cup graham cracker crumbs *or* 4 large graham crackers, finely crushed
- ¼ cup granulated sugar
- 2 medium Gala apples, cut into 8 wedges each

CARAMEL SAUCE

- ½ cup packed brown sugar
- ¼ cup whipping cream
- 2 tablespoons butter
- 2 tablespoons light corn syrup
- ¼ teaspoon salt

1 Place flour in shallow dish. Beat eggs in another shallow dish. Combine graham cracker crumbs and granulated sugar in third shallow dish.

2 Coat apple wedges with flour. Dip in eggs, letting excess drip back into dish. Roll apples in graham cracker crumb mixture to coat. Place on baking sheet or large plate; refrigerate 15 to 30 minutes.

3 Preheat air fryer to 390°F. Line basket with parchment paper.

4 Cook apples 6 to 8 minutes or until slightly tender and golden brown.

5 For sauce, combine brown sugar, cream, butter, corn syrup and salt in small saucepan; cook and stir over medium-low heat until well blended and heated through. Serve with apple fries.

Makes 6 servings

Chocolate Orange Lava Cakes

½ cup semisweet chocolate chips

¼ cup (½ stick) butter

½ cup powdered sugar, plus additional for garnish

2 eggs

2 egg yolks

½ teaspoon orange extract

¼ teaspoon salt

3 tablespoons all-purpose flour

Candied or grated orange peel (optional)

1 Preheat air fryer to 370°F. Spray four 4-ounce ramekins with nonstick cooking spray.

2 Combine chocolate chips and butter in medium microwavable bowl; microwave on HIGH 45 seconds. Stir until mixture is melted and smooth. Add ½ cup powdered sugar, eggs, egg yolks, orange extract and salt; stir until well blended. Stir in flour just until blended. Pour batter into prepared ramekins.

3 Cook 10 to 12 minutes or until set. Remove ramekins to wire rack to cool 15 minutes.

4 Run knife around edges of cakes to loosen. Invert cakes onto plates; invert again onto serving plates. Sprinkle with additional powdered sugar; garnish with orange peel.

Makes 4 servings

Tropical Pineapple Rings

1 can (20 ounces) pineapple slices in juice

1 teaspoon coconut extract

2 eggs

½ cup all-purpose flour

1 cup panko bread crumbs

1 cup unsweetened shredded coconut

  Maraschino cherries (optional)

1 Drain pineapple, reserving ¾ cup juice. Place pineapple in large resealable food storage bag; add ¼ cup reserved pineapple juice and coconut extract. Seal bag; refrigerate at least 15 minutes.

2 Beat eggs and remaining ½ cup pineapple juice in shallow dish. Place flour in another shallow dish. Combine panko and coconut in third shallow dish.

3 Drain pineapple; discard juice. Pat slices dry with paper towels.

4 Coat pineapple with flour. Dip in egg mixture, letting excess drip back into dish, then coat with panko mixture. Place pineapple on baking sheet; refrigerate 15 minutes.

5 Preheat air fryer to 350°F. Spray basket with nonstick cooking spray.

6 Cook pineapple in batches 5 to 6 minutes or until coating is crisp and lightly browned. Serve warm; garnish with cherries.

Makes 10 servings

Apple Pie Pockets

2 pieces lavash bread, each cut into 4 rectangles

2 tablespoons melted butter

¾ cup apple pie filling

1 egg

1 teaspoon water

½ cup powdered sugar

⅛ teaspoon ground cinnamon

2½ teaspoons milk

1 Brush one side of each piece of lavash with butter. Place four pieces buttered side down on work surface. Spoon 3 tablespoons pie filling in center of each piece, leaving ½-inch border.

2 Beat egg and water in small bowl. Brush border of lavash pieces around filling with egg mixture; top with remaining lavash pieces, buttered side up. Press edges together with fork to seal. Cut 3 small slits in center of each pocket with paring knife.

3 Preheat air fryer to 370°F. Line basket with parchment paper.

4 Cook pockets in batches 8 to 10 minutes or until golden brown and crisp. Remove to wire rack to cool 15 minutes.

5 Whisk powdered sugar, cinnamon and milk in small bowl until smooth. Drizzle glaze over pockets; let stand 15 minutes to allow glaze to set.

Makes 4 servings

METRIC CONVERSION CHART

VOLUME MEASUREMENTS (dry)

⅛ teaspoon = 0.5 mL
¼ teaspoon = 1 mL
½ teaspoon = 2 mL
¾ teaspoon = 4 mL
1 teaspoon = 5 mL
1 tablespoon = 15 mL
2 tablespoons = 30 mL
¼ cup = 60 mL
⅓ cup = 75 mL
½ cup = 125 mL
⅔ cup = 150 mL
¾ cup = 175 mL
1 cup = 250 mL
2 cups = 1 pint = 500 mL
3 cups = 750 mL
4 cups = 1 quart = 1 L

VOLUME MEASUREMENTS (fluid)

1 fluid ounce (2 tablespoons) = 30 mL
4 fluid ounces (½ cup) = 125 mL
8 fluid ounces (1 cup) = 250 mL
12 fluid ounces (1½ cups) = 375 mL
16 fluid ounces (2 cups) = 500 mL

WEIGHTS (mass)

½ ounce = 15 g
1 ounce = 30 g
3 ounces = 90 g
4 ounces = 120 g
8 ounces = 225 g
10 ounces = 285 g
12 ounces = 360 g
16 ounces = 1 pound = 450 g

DIMENSIONS

1/16 inch = 2 mm
⅛ inch = 3 mm
¼ inch = 6 mm
½ inch = 1.5 cm
¾ inch = 2 cm
1 inch = 2.5 cm

OVEN TEMPERATURES

250°F = 120°C
275°F = 140°C
300°F = 150°C
325°F = 160°C
350°F = 180°C
375°F = 190°C
400°F = 200°C
425°F = 220°C
450°F = 230°C

BAKING PAN SIZES

Utensil	Size in Inches/Quarts	Metric Volume	Size in Centimeters
Baking or Cake Pan (square or rectangular)	8×8×2	2 L	20×20×5
	9×9×2	2.5 L	23×23×5
	12×8×2	3 L	30×20×5
	13×9×2	3.5 L	33×23×5
Loaf Pan	8×4×3	1.5 L	20×10×7
	9×5×3	2 L	23×13×7
Round Layer Cake Pan	8×1½	1.2 L	20×4
	9×1½	1.5 L	23×4
Pie Plate	8×1¼	750 mL	20×3
	9×1¼	1 L	23×3
Baking Dish or Casserole	1 quart	1 L	—
	1½ quart	1.5 L	—
	2 quart	2 L	—